THE HUMBLE DIVINITY OF JESUS

IN MARK'S GOSPEL
Vol.1 (chs.1 to 9)

DANIEL BOURGUET

Foreword by BOB EKBLAD

Translated by ROGER WILKINSON

THE PEOPLE'S SEMINARY PRESS

The Humble Divinity of Jesus

The People's Seminary Press
Burlington, WA 98233
www.peoplesseminary.org
ISBN: 978-1-954387-03-4

Bible passages are literal translations of the French. The author uses a range of French translations.

CONTENTS

Translator's note

In some instances there are idioms in French that are difficult to translate, but that has not generally been the case with this great book. The French text doesn't have any notes so all footnotes are the translator's; sometimes these are glosses on the French, sometimes of a more explanatory nature; these notes have been implicitly endorsed by Daniel Bourguet. Passages from the Bible are mostly the translator's version of the French since at times the point would be lost if this were not so; DB chooses freely among French translations.

The author's preferences when it comes to capitalizing, particularly with pronouns that refer to God have always been followed.

In keeping with the other translations in this series, a substantial effort has been made to employ "gender neutral" terms. Sensitivity in this area is not something that is found in French in general and not in the original text of these books so the neutrality hasn't always been easy. This is particularly true when it comes to Biblical quotations.

FOREWORD

THE PUBLICATION OF DANIEL BOURGUET'S BOOKS IN
English is a valuable contribution to the literature of
contemplative theology and spirituality that will nourish
and inspire the faith of all who read them. Daniel Bourguet,
a French Protestant pastor and theologian of the Huguenot
tradition, lives as a monk in the mountainous Cévennes
region in the south of France. There at his hermitage near
Saint-Jean-du-Gard, Daniel maintains a daily rhythm of
prayer, worship, Scripture reading, theological reflection,
and spiritual accompaniment. All of his books flow out of
a life steeped in love of God, Scripture, and the seekers who
come to him for spiritual support.

I first met Daniel Bourguet in 1988 when my wife,
Gracie, and I moved from rural Central America to study
theology at the Institut Protestant de Théologie (IPT),
where he taught Old Testament. The IPT is the Église
Réformée de France's[1] denominational graduate school in
Montpellier, France.

Prior to our move to France, while ministering among
impoverished farmers in Honduras in the 1980s, we
came across the writings of the Swiss theologian Wilhelm

1. Now Église Protestante Unie de France.

Vischer and the French theologian Daniel Lys by way of footnotes in Jacques Ellul's inspiring books. Vischer had written a three-volume work entitled *The Witness of the Old Testament to Christ*, of which only volume 1 is translated into English.[2] That book, along with a number of articles and Daniel Lys' brilliant *The Meaning of the Old Testament*,[3] exposed us to a community of Bible scholars who articulated a continuity between the Old and New Testaments that was highly relevant both then and now. This connection ultimately led me to Bourguet.

We experienced firsthand how a literal reading of the Old Testament in isolation from the New Testament confession that Jesus is both Lord and Christ (Messiah) brings great confusion, division, and even destruction. In rural Honduras churches often distinguish themselves by selectively observing Old Testament laws and using certain Old Testament stories to inspire fear of God as a punishing judge. North American Christians at this time were drawing from the Old Testament to justify the death penalty and US military intervention in Central America and beyond.

Wilhelm Vischer, an active resister of Nazism from his Old Testament teaching post inside Germany, resisted the misuse of Scripture to justify anti-Semitism, nationalism, and war, insisting on the importance of the Old Testament for Christian faith at a time when it was being dismissed. He was consequently one of the first professors of theology to be pressured to leave his post and eventually depart Nazi Germany before World War II. He served as Karl

2. Wilhelm Vischer, *The Witness of the Old Testament to Christ*, vol. 1, *The Pentateuch*, trans. A. B. Crabtree (London: Lutterworth, 1949).

3. Daniel Lys, *The Meaning of the Old Testament* (Nashville: Abingdon, 1967).

Barth's pastor in Basel after he, too, left Germany. After the war, the church in France, having been widely engaged in resistance to Nazism and deeply encouraged by Barth, invited Vischer to be the professor of Old Testament at the IPT in Montpellier.

The biblical reflections of Ellul, Vischer, Lys and other French theologians led Gracie and I to look into theological study in France.[4] We wrote the IPT about their graduate program and discovered that Vischer had long since retired after training several generations of pastors. His protégée, Daniel Lys, had recently retired but was still available. Lys's place had been filled by his doctoral student, Daniel Bourguet, who also had been trained by Vischer. The IPT welcomed us with a generous scholarship, and we soon made plans to learn French and move to Montpellier.

After being immersed in Bible studies with impoverished farmers in war-torn Honduras, we were eager for help in understanding Scripture. Disillusioned with America after being engaged in resisting US policy in Central America, we felt drawn to reflect from a different context. We reasoned that studying in a Protestant seminary with a history of persecution in a majority Catholic context would prove valuable. We left Tierra Nueva in the hands of local Honduran leaders and moved to Montpellier in July 1988 to study French and then began classes in September

Daniel Bourguet taught us Hebrew and Old Testament in ways that made the language and text come alive. He invited students into his passion and curiosity as we

4. We assumed there were others where these came from, and were able to study with pastor and New Testament professor Michel Bouttier, who was also trained by Vischer and published broadly, including a commentary on Ephesians and a number of collections of provocative articles. Elian Cuvillier followed Bouttier as Professor of New Testament at the IPT, writing many high quality books and articles.

pondered both familiar and difficult passages of Scripture. I remember continually being surprised at how seriously Daniel took every textual critical variant, even seemingly irrelevant ones. He masterfully invited and guided us to both scrutinize and contemplate each variant in its original language until we understood the angle from which ancient interpreters had viewed the text. Daniel modeled an honoring of distinct perspectives as we studied the history of interpretation of each passage. He sought to hold diverse perspectives together whenever possible, yet only embraced what the text actually permitted, exemplifying fine-tuned discernment that inspired us.

Daniel's thorough approach meant he would only take us through a chapter or two per semester. This mean we took entire courses on Genesis 1–2:4, on Abraham's call in Genesis 12:1-4, and on Jeremiah 31, Exodus 1–2, Psalms 1–2 and others. In each of his courses he included relevant rabbinic exegesis, New Testament use of the Old Testament, and the church fathers' interpretations. Daniel imparted his confidence that God speaks good news now as he accompanied us in our reading, making our hearts burn like those of the disciples of Emmaus, and inspiring us to want to do this with others. In alignment with Vischer and Lys he demonstrated through detailed exegesis of Old Testament texts how God's most total revelation in Jesus both fulfills and explains these Scriptures, making them come alive through the Holy Spirit in our lives and diverse contexts.

While living in France, Gracie and I traveled to Honduras every summer, spending several weeks sharing our learning with Tierra Nueva's Honduran leadership and leading Bible studies in rural villages before returning for classes in the fall. We pursued our studies in France with the vision of bringing the best scholarship to the service of the least in a deliberate effort to bridge the divide between the academy and the poor. Our experience of Daniel's rare blend of scholarship and pastoral sensitivity, which you will see for yourself in his books, contributed to us feeling called back to the church, into ordained ministry, and back to the US to teach and minister there. I benefited from having Daniel as my dissertation supervisor and continued to integrate regular study into our ministry of accompanying immigrants and inmates when we launched Tierra Nueva in Washington State.

Daniel Bourguet's writings are like high-quality wine extracted from vineyards planted in challenged soil. Born in 1946 in Aumessas, a small village in the Cévennes region of France, Daniel grew up in the heartland of Huguenot Protestantism, which issued from the Reformation in the sixteenth century. He pursued studies of theology at the IPT in Montpellier, including study in Germany, Switzerland and at the Ecole Biblique in Jerusalem. In lieu of military service, Daniel served as a teacher in Madagascar for a year. He was ordained as a pastor in the Église Réformée de France in 1972, serving parishes from 1973 to 1987. Daniel wrote his doctoral dissertation[5] while serving as a full-time parish pastor—a common practice in minority Protestant France, where teaching positions are scarce and pastors are in high demand. This practice often proves fruitful for ordinary Christians and theologians alike, deepening reflection and anchoring theologians in the church and world.

During our residential studies in Montpellier from 1988 to 1991, Gracie and I witnessed Daniel's interest in the early monastics and fathers of the Eastern Church grow. In 1991 Daniel became prior of La Fraternité Spirituelle des

5. See Daniel Bourguet, Des métaphores de Jérémie, Paris : J. Gabalda, 1987

Veilleurs (Spiritual Fraternity of the Watchpersons) and felt called to be a full-time monk, leaving the IPT in 1995 for a year in a Cistercian monastery in Lyon before moving to his current site in Les Cévennes in 1996.

Joy, simplicity, and mercy are the three pillars of Les Veilleurs, an association of laypeople and pastors founded by French Reformed pastor Wilfred Monod in 1923 (with a Francophone membership of four hundred in 2013). Members of this fellowship commit to pursuing daily rhythms of prayer and Scripture reading, including noontime recitation of the Beatitudes, Friday meditation on the cross, regular engagement with a faith community on Sundays, and spiritual retreats and reading that benefits from universal devotional and monastic practices. Les Veilleurs has served to nourish renewal in France and influenced the founding of communities such as Taizé. Under Daniel Bourguet's leadership Les Veilleurs thrived. As a member of Les Veilleurs myself I attended many of his annual retreats, witnessing and experiencing the vitality of this movement firsthand.

Since Daniel's departure from his professorship at the IPT in 1995, his teaching and writing have focused primarily on equipping ordinary Christians to grow spiritually through engaging in devotional practices such as prayer, Scripture reading and contemplation. Other works that will hopefully appear in English include reflections on asceticism, silence, daily prayer and the Trinity. All but three of Daniel's twenty-five or so books are based on spiritual retreats he offered to pastors and retreatants with Les Veilleurs. He has offered retreats to Roman Catholic, Orthodox, and Protestant communities throughout France and Francophone Europe and is widely read and appreciated as a theologian who bridges divergent worlds and nourishes faithful Christian practice in France. Daniel Bourguet made his first and only visit to the United States in 2005, offering a spiritual retreat in Washington State. He accompanied me to Honduras on that same trip just after Hurricane Katrina ravaged the country, teaching Tierra Nueva's leaders and accompanying me as I led Bible studies and ministered in rural communities.

Daniel left his role as prior in 2012 and now continues his daily offices, receives many seekers for personal retreats, and offers occasional retreats where he lives and writes. In alignment with the early monastic commitment to manual labor, Daniel weaves black and white wool tapestries of illustrations of biblical stories done by pastor and painter Henri Lindegaard. Daniel's unique contribution includes his Trinitarian approach to biblical interpretation, wherein he reads Scripture informed by the early church fathers with special sensitivity to how texts bear witness directly and indirectly to Jesus, the Father and the Holy Spirit.

Daniel Bourguet models an approach to Scripture and spirituality that is desperately needed in our times. He reads the Bible with great confidence in God's goodness, discovering through careful reading, prayer, and contemplation insights that feed faith and inspire practice. Daniel's deliberate reading in communion with the church fathers brings the wisdom of the ages to nourish the body of Christ today. His tender love for people who come to him for spiritual support as well as the larger church and world informs every page of his writing. May you find in this book refreshment, strength, and inspiration for your journey as you are drawn into deeper encounters with God.

Bob Ekblad
Mount Vernon, WA

PREFACE

This book is the material from a retreat given a number of times in the course of 2019 at *Les Abeillères* to different groups; I would like to express my thankfulness to these groups because their various reactions have been very precious as I have corrected and clarified.

In retreats, as with preaching, bibliographic references are left to one side; they might have had a place in marginal notes, but I have preferred to keep them to a minimum in order to stay close to the style of a retreat, as if the reader was taking part in a retreat through this book.

The people present at these retreats were believers, Christians, and the reader will see that my remarks assume this. Nothing has been changed here, so a reader who is not a believer will undoubtedly feel uncomfortable at times; for the host of questions that will arise for such a reader I ask pardon; however, to go on a retreat is to retire from the world for a time to be face to face with God and the teaching at a retreat is a means to that encounter; for this, a person would have to be a believer. You need to know this before starting to read the book; I am speaking here as if at a retreat, to a reader who is a believer.

Finally, again as if on a retreat, I have kept the elements of an oral style. You are addressed here as a "reader friend," in the form of a dialogue, a dialogue which is intended to be no more than an overture to the most sublime of dialogues, dialogue with God.

So there we are, my reader friend! May your dialogue with God find something here to nourish it.

INTRODUCTION

I AM NOT A SPECIALIST IN MARK'S GOSPEL, WHICH MEANS I simply accept the view of the great majority of those who are that this gospel is the oldest of the four. Matthew and Luke, in fact, seem to have leant on Mark rather than the other way round. As for John, the most original of the four, his would seem to be the most recent gospel.

Mark is considered to have been a Jewish Christian, given his excellent knowledge of the Old Testament and of Jewish practices. It's thought today that he was writing for Latins, and more precisely for the Christians in Rome. The reason we can say this is that he was speaking to people who did not know Aramean, the tongue spoken in Israel, so he needed to translate Aramean expressions such as *talitha qoum* ("little girl, arise" (5:41)), éphphatha ("be opened" (7:34)) or *Abba* ("Father" (14:36)). Similarly, we can tell he was addressing Latin speakers because he gives the Latin equivalent of the two *leptes* (a Greek coin) given by a widow (12:42), saying that was equal to a *quadran* (a Roman coin); or again, he uses the word *praetorium*, from the Latin, to designate the interior of Pilate's palace (15:16).

If Mark was writing in Rome, it's because he had followed Peter, who finished his life there, undoubtedly in the year 64. In about 110, Papias, the bishop of Hierapolis, tells us that Mark was "Peter's interpreter," which fits with what Peter himself wrote, speaking of Mark as his "son who is in Babylon" (that is, Rome; 1 Pet 5:13). Certainly Mark found his main source of information for his gospel in Peter, and we have evidence of this in the large place he has in the gospel.

Furthermore, Mark's presence in Rome would also be because of his association with Paul, who also finished his life there, in about the year 67. The book of Acts (12:21, 25; 15:37, 39), as well as Paul himself in his letters (2 Tim 4:11, Phlm 24), tell us of one Mark, "his co-worker," who is generally considered to be the author of the gospel. And it is true that in this gospel we find a deep influence from Paul's theology.

In brief, basing my views on the specialists, I believe that Mark was a Jew who had spent a great deal of time with Peter and Paul. He was not one of the twelve but he had been formed and marked by Peter, who was a direct witness of the life of Christ, and by Paul with respect to theological reflection. This is as much as to say that Mark was well placed to write his gospel. As we read, we realize that Mark manages a sort of synthesis of what he received from Peter and Paul, and he integrates with this his own meditation of the Old Testament and all the Holy Spirit gave him in his prayerful reading of the Scriptures.

Influenced then by Peter and Paul, Mark had acquired a real authority, and this explains why Matthew and Luke were inspired by him to write their gospels. In Matthew's case it is most surprising that he, one of the Twelve, should be inspired by Mark when he wrote. This tells us the extent to which Mark became authoritative.

Why write a gospel?

Why then did Mark set pen to paper? In particular, it was because Peter and Paul had recently died. With the death of these two great witnesses of nascent Christianity, it became important to write down and collect, in the light of Paul's theology, the information received from Peter about Jesus.

With Peter and Paul alive, it wouldn't have seemed important to write; there was still a literal understanding of the following saying of Jesus' about the end times: "In truth I tell you that this generation will not pass away before this all takes place" (13:30). Now though, the generation of Peter and Paul was indeed passing away, and the end had not come; and so it was that Mark began to write, the spiritual son of Peter and co-laborer with Paul, for the edification of the generations to come. I am unaware if Mark wrote on his own initiative or if he had been asked to do so by the Christians in Rome, in mourning for the two great apostles. At all events, he seems to have written before the year 79, which was the date of the sack of Jerusalem, to which he does not allude.

When Mark wrote, the church in Rome had been going through a real trauma; following the burning of Rome in 64, the emperor Nero had arrested Christians and persecuted them harshly on the pretext that they were responsible for the catastrophe.

I understand this to be the context which gave birth to the first gospel; Mark wrote addressing a community in mourning for Peter, Paul and the victims of Nero, to a community in great suffering and doubtless shaken in their faith by the loss of the first generation of Christians. Mark began writing in an endeavor to console, comfort and edify his readers. He did so by setting forth the perfect humanity and the perfect divinity of Jesus according to all he had heard both from Peter and Paul, and from the Holy Spirit in the course of his own meditations in the Scriptures.

"He who was crucified is risen," the women were told on the last page of the gospel (16:6). They were also told that the Risen One was going ahead of the disciples, to their homes, and while this concerns the first generation disciples, it is also pertinent to every generation to come. The One who brings all generations together is revealed on each page of the gospel, in his perfect humanity, in his beneficent nearness, as he accompanies the disciples through their daily lives in his perfect divinity to reassure and strengthen them, even when a tempest such as Nero's rages. He is there, fully God, the one whom even the wind and the sea obey (4:41). It is he who is revealed in Mark's gospel.

Today, the perfect humanity of Christ does not need emphasizing since so many books are devoted to the theme, and rightly so; by contrast, the divinity of Christ does seem to me less considered, and this impels me to want to focus here, without of course in any way impugning his perfect humanity.

If we have difficulty today perceiving the divinity of Jesus, it seems to me this is because he is humble, and in our eyes humility is incompatible with the glory of divinity. It's certainly true that Jesus is humble, and I would say doubly so, humble in his humanity as well as in his divinity because God himself is humble. This is unacceptable to anyone who thinks that God cannot be both glorious and humble. What exactly though is glory? If the most glorious of kings combines pride with his glory, the pride will tarnish the glory and diminish it. However, if he is humble, his humility embellishes and enhances his glory. Humility combines wonderfully with glory. To say that God is humble takes away nothing from his glory; on the contrary, it elevates and makes it still more magnificent. The perfect humility of Jesus beautifies his humanity and his divinity as well. On this basis, we mustn't be given pause by Jesus' humility but should rather welcome it as a quality which both hides and reveals his divinity.

Mark the contemplative

A striking feature of Mark's gospel is its great sobriety; it's certainly very succinct. To me, this shows Mark had no wish to invent but wanted to hold humbly and strictly to what he had received from Peter, Paul and certain other witnesses of Christ he had met. His great sobriety also shows that Mark had well understood that the divine-humanity of Christ is a real mystery which takes us deep into the inexpressible since, in his divinity, Jesus is beyond anything we could say of him. None of our human languages is sufficient to speak of God and the divinity of Jesus. To mitigate this deficiency in words, Mark is content to work by suggestion, to evoke this mystery which is far beyond us but neverthelesss offered for our contemplation. The sobriety seems to me to belong to a contemplative, and this indeed appears to be Mark's nature, a contemplative open to the inexpressible, open and sensitive to the mystery of God. In passing on as he does the fruits of his contemplation, Mark conveys all he had been granted to perceive of the perfect divinity of Christ but without overlooking anything of his perfect humanity.

I find Mark interesting in that like us he had not met Jesus, and so, like us, depended on the witness of others and had to learn to trust them. He interests me most particularly in this area of helping us to open ourselves to contemplate the mystery of the divine-humanity of Jesus.

How paradoxical, that Mark should contemplate Jesus though he had never seen him! It's true though, and it's the same for us; to contemplate does not mean fixing our eyes physically on Christ, on his visible humanity, but our inner eyes on his invisible divinity as it is seen through his full humanity. This is a gift of the Holy Spirit.

What I am proposing, reader friend, is to pause over certain texts in Mark's gospel, following Mark in his contemplation of the divinity of Jesus. To do so, we have to accept that Mark, no more than anyone else, proves that Jesus is God. It is a fact to say that the divinity of Jesus is not demonstrable; it is not susceptible of proof by human reasoning. To believe in the divinity of Christ is a gift of the Spirit granted to faith. Our place is to receive this mystery in faith and to celebrate Christ in praises which exceed words. This was Mark's experience, writing his gospel as an expression and even a celebration of his faith, to help us to live out our faith. He wrote to comfort a Roman community shaken in its faith. By the Holy Spirit, we in turn can be edified and strengthened in faith thanks to this gospel.

The divinity of Jesus appears with varying degrees of clarity in the passages of the gospel. Before we look at particular accounts, we will review a few of the places where it is indicated most plainly.

In the passage of Jesus walking on the sea, Jesus reassured and comforted the disciples as they struggled through the storm, telling them, "It is I" (égô eïmi, 6:50). Word for word he said, "I am," which, for the disciples as Jews, was very clear: only God speaks like this since this is the way he presented himself to Moses: "I am the one who is" (Exod 3:14). In the Hellenistic Judaism of the beginning of our era to say not only, "I am the one who is," but merely, "I am" was enough to be considered blasphemous; speaking like this was to take oneself for God. This is why when Jesus said again, "I am," before the Sanhedrin (14:62), the high priest rose up and denounced it as blasphemy (14:63–64). For the high priest, Jesus was a blasphemer, but for the disciples things were very different. In the boat, far from protesting, they were silent before this man walking on the sea and saying to them, "I am." They received these words which revealed to them a most profound mystery; in silence, they contemplated Jesus appearing to them in his divinity! That a man would be God — what an unfathomable mystery! To help the reader understand, Mark underlines the divinity of Jesus by using the expression "walk on the sea" just as it is found used of God and of God alone in the Old Testament (Job 9:8).

In order to strengthen his readers' faith in the divinity of Jesus, Mark points in that direction from the outset of his gospel. In fact, the gospel opens with a quotation from the prophet Isaiah, "Prepare the way of the Lord" (40:3). All that follows in the gospel shows that the Lord announced is indeed Jesus. To refer to Jesus as "the Lord" is itself a revelation of his divinity. If we go back to the verse from Isaiah, we find that the word used there for "Lord" corresponds to the tetragram (YHWH), which is a title for God. Our verse says, "Prepare the way of God." Those of Mark's readers who didn't know Hebrew and might hesitate over the meaning of "Lord" would easily perceive that "the Lord" Isaiah talks about must be God, not some human lord. In fact, in terms of the context in Isaiah, "prepare the way of the Lord" meant preparing the way of the God of Israel, who would return from Babylon with the exiles of his people. "Prepare the way of the Lord": this is how Mark points to Jesus as God. It's not only John the Baptist in the opening chapter who announces the divinity of Jesus; the prophet Isaiah had already announced it. The divinity of Jesus does not need to be demonstrated; it had already been announced and revealed by an Old Testament prophet.

"The beginning of the gospel of Jesus Christ, Son of God" (1:1).[1] We're not looking closely at the title of the gospel, but it does require one comment. Its last words, "Son of God," speak clearly of Jesus' divinity, though it does pose a problem because we don't find it in every manuscript. The oldest manuscripts we have today date from the 4th and 5th centuries: the Sinaiticus, the Alexandrinus, the Vaticanus, Codex Ephraemi and the Codex Bezae. The expression "Son of God" is attested by Vaticanus and Codex Bezae, but not by the other three; this is not strong attestation. If the phrase is Mark's, it faithfully conveys his thoughts on the divinity of Jesus Christ; if, however, it was added by scribe, we might remark that he had properly understood Mark's thinking! Whatever the case, it is an accurate reflection of the gospel's contents, and it is magnificent for us today to read in our translations, in this opening verse: "Jesus Christ, Son of God."

A few verses further on, when it comes to Jesus' baptism, God speaks, and he says to Jesus, "You are my beloved Son" (1:11). Here we have God the Father revealed to us speaking to his Son, who is himself God. To lead us further into the contemplation of the mystery of God, Father and Son, the account of Jesus' baptism relates the gentle descent onto him of the Holy Spirit like a dove (1:10). Mark then suspends his account immediately after these words spoken by the Father to his Son, leaving us with a sense that the account is incomplete. This feeling of incompleteness no doubt has to do with Mark not knowing what to say after mentioning the Father, the Son and the Holy Spirit. He falls silent, finding himself before the inexpressible mystery of the Trinity. He suspends his account to contemplate: the

1. Translating the French. There is no article before "Son" in numerous French translations, or in the Greek.

Father speaking to the Son in the gentleness of the Holy Spirit . . .

The baptism account takes up only 3 verses! Right here we see Mark's sobriety: 3 verses only to evoke the presence of the Trinity! This is the sobriety of contemplatives.

Mark's gospel therefore opens not with the birth of Jesus as in the gospels of Matthew and Luke, but with a presentation of Jesus in his divinity, the Jesus who from his first appearing, from his baptism, is offered up to our contemplation with the Father and the Holy Spirit in the unfathomable mystery of the Trinity. Mark is not proving to us the divinity of Christ or the Trinity; he just soberly opens up before us mysteries which he offers for our contemplation, mysteries which he suggests throughout his gospel.

Reader friend, it's in this vein that I invite you to follow Mark in all he proposes for our meditation and contemplation. It's superfluous to say that I tremble; before Jesus and his divine-humanity, it could not be otherwise. May God bless us and help us in our reading and meditation of the gospel.

O heavenly King, Comforter, Spirit of truth, you who are present everywhere, filling all things, treasure of good and giver of life, come and abide in us, cleanse us of every stain and save our souls, you who are kind.

THE PARALYTIC

(Mark 2:1-12)

1. He came again to Capernaum a few days later. It became known that he was in a certain house, 2. and many people assembled so that there was no room, not even by the door. He spoke the Word to them. 3. A paralytic was brought to him, carried by four men, 4. but because they were unable to get to him because of the crowd, they uncovered the tiles from the roof where he was, and, after making an opening, they let down the bed on which the paralytic man lay. 5. Jesus, seeing their faith, said to the paralytic: "My child, your sins are forgiven."

6. Some scribes were seated there, and they reasoned in their hearts, 7. "Why does this fellow speak like this? He is blaspheming. Who can forgive sins except God alone?" 8. Immediately, knowing in his spirit that they were reasoning in this way, Jesus said to them, "Why are you reasoning like this in your hearts? 9. Which is easier to say to the paralytic, 'Your sins are forgiven,' or 'Rise, take up your bed and walk'? So that you may know that the Son of Man has authority on earth to forgive sins, (he said to the paralytic) I say to you, Rise, take up your bed and go to your house." 12. He arose (=he was raised) *and immediately picking up his bed, he walked out in front of them all, so that they were all amazed and glorified God, saying, "We've never seen anything like it."*

WHILE JESUS IS THE CENTRAL CHARACTER IN THE PASSAGE, most surprisingly we see that Mark delays naming him. Jesus is present from the first verse, but his name is not mentioned, and instead he is referred to by pronouns: "He came . . ., he was . . ., was led to him . . ." This procedure of Mark's has not sat easy with translators; to make the account clearer they have allowed themselves to add Jesus' name, commonly in the first verse.[2] We will stay with the Greek text, which doesn't mention Jesus by name until verse 5.

With this delay in introducing Jesus' name, I believe that Mark simply wishes us to understand that up to verse 5 events are merely preparatory and that the most important element is what follows. The opening is picturesque and even a little bizarre with the arrival of the paralytic down through an opening in the roof. Mark describes it all with plenty of details, but it's not what is really important to him. In verse 2, he also tells us that Jesus was preaching, which is not without interest, but Mark tells us nothing of what was said. "He spoke the Word to them," he tells us simply. Very evidently, Mark's interest is elsewhere. The first words of Jesus we are told about are those addressed to the paralytic, and this immediately follows the mention of Jesus' name in a very striking expression, "Jesus, seeing

2. DB cites three French translations. The same is true in many English versions, though not the KJV.

2

their faith" (v 5). This is the point at which, for Mark, the important events begin. It's where I will start.

"Seeing their faith"

"Jesus, seeing their faith": this expression must surely hold our attention, to begin with because it's the first time Mark names Jesus in this passage, but also because it's the only time in the whole gospel that there is a faith which is visible. The phrasing is so strong that in their parallel accounts Matthew and Luke both make use of it, while they either change or leave out many other similar expressions. Nowhere else in the four gospels or in the rest of the New Testament is there faith which can be seen. The closest is in James, which says to "show your faith." [3]

"Jesus, seeing their faith": to bring a sharper emphasis to this, Mark, in his account to this point, has carefully described many things that can be seen, things that are rather striking, particularly the arrival of the paralytic man through the roof. To see all this, however, was simply a physical matter. The opening events are easy to describe: a house packed with people, some men making a hole in the roof and then lowering a stretcher with a paralyzed man lying on it. We can imagine all this. But after the descriptive passage, Mark passes from the visible to the invisible, to the unseen seen only by Jesus: "He saw faith"! I believe that in so doing, Mark is drawing our attention to Jesus and to a most singular Jesus, one who "sees faith." This would seem to be a trait of divinity. Who indeed sees faith except for God? We find God himself saying in the Old Testament, "Man looks on the outward appearance, but the Lord sees the heart" (1 Sam 16:7). This is what is happening here

---

3. Although Acts 14:9: "Seeing that he had faith to be healed."

because in the Bible faith is in the heart. If Jesus saw faith, it means he was seeing into the heart in a way only God can.

I am struck by the simplicity with which Mark points to the divinity of Jesus. "Jesus, seeing their faith": just a few words, with no commentary, and that was enough. Reader friend, it is good to be at home with this sort of discretion, the discretion of contemplatives, who prefer to suggest rather than state openly. Mark evokes things, suggesting them, not wanting to misrepresent with superfluous words the one he is contemplating in his divinity.

Jesus, Mark tells us, saw "their faith," without specifying the nature of the faith. In context, the issue is the faith of the four men carrying the bed, doing all they could to get the paralytic to Jesus. Are we also talking about the faith of the paralytic? Ancient commentators, the Church Fathers, are divided on this point. Ephrem, in the 4th century, thought it was just the faith of the four (*Commentary on the Diatessaron*). However, most other Fathers thought the paralytic's faith is indicated too, given that he must certainly have been fully party to the project of encountering Jesus. Thus John Chrysostom in the 4th century (*Sermons on the gospel of St Matthew,* 29/1), and Barsanaphius in the 6th century (Letter 387). I too believe that Jesus saw the faith of the four and of the man himself, united in their mutual project.

"Seeing their faith": Mark's wording is so succinct that it is difficult to know whether we have in view faith in God or faith in Jesus. Through the rest of the gospel, Jesus does invite faith in God (11:22), but generally, the imprecision remains (4:40; 5:34; 10:52). In each of these passages, the faith could either be in God or in Jesus. If we base our thinking on Mark having received from Paul, it is possible to think in terms of faith in Jesus (cf Phil 1:29). That these men's actions involved turning to Jesus, wouldn't this suggest they were placing faith in him? Whatever the case, I ask myself if Mark wasn't keeping the ambiguity and letting us think that it was faith in God and in Jesus. For Mark, in fact, Jesus himself is God, so we do well to believe that faith in God and faith in Jesus are one and the same thing. Isn't this along the same lines as we find in John's gospel, where Jesus himself says to his disciples, "You believe in God, believe also in me" (14:1)? That these men were laying the paralytic before Jesus is surely a sign of believing in God and in Jesus. Mark is so discreet, no more than suggesting the implicit divinity of Jesus.

"Seeing their faith": in what way was the faith perceptible? Perhaps the expression will be clearer to us if we can grasp what exactly enabled Jesus to see the men's faith. How was he able to perceive it? Perhaps it's that nothing prevented the four men carrying through their plan? They were certainly so determined in their faith that nothing would stand in their way of getting to Jesus, to the point of breaking up the roof of the house. Perhaps it was their love for the paralyzed man, the love that hopes all things, that bears all things, that "believes all things," according to Paul (1 Cor 13:7)? Was it this that made their faith visible to Jesus? Perhaps! However, what makes me dubious, hesitant, and is rather striking is to consider what becomes of this passage in Matthew.

Matthew tells us this when he opens his account: "After getting into a boat, he crossed the sea and came to his hometown. There, a paralytic was brought to him, lying on a bed" (9:1–2). That's it! Then Matthew continues, "Jesus, seeing their faith". It's surely surprising that nothing is said of the hole in the roof. Even the four friends are not mentioned, and Matthew limits himself to a simple, "He was brought," which is not precise at all. The rather spectacular arrival of the paralyzed man is gone, indeed everything that could make the faith of the people involved visible. Despite this, Matthew stays with the fact that Jesus "saw their faith" (9:3). What was there visible about their faith in Matthew's account? Matthew just keeps one element, that the men "brought" (*prosphérô*) the paralytic to Jesus. Where Mark tells us this, he does so insistently: firstly "they brought him" (*phérô pros,* 2:3), and then "unable to bring him to him" (*prosphérô*).

In what sense does bringing the paralytic to Jesus make faith visible? In an earlier passage, Mark tells us that the sick were brought (*phérô pros* 1:32) to Jesus. The wording is the same, but nothing is said of the faith of the sick people or of those who brought them! Nothing is said of Jesus being particularly sensitive to anything! Later, little children were brought (*prosphérô* 10:13) to him, but again nothing is said of the faith of anyone involved.

I believe that the question of knowing how Jesus managed to see faith is beyond our understanding. Perhaps it's part of the mystery of Jesus that he should be able to see people's faith while we are unable. Perhaps it is a trait of his divinity. At all events, nothing in the letters of Peter or Paul will help us to understand this expression in Mark, an expression Mark himself does not explain.

However, Paul does help us make some progress on this issue, shedding some light from a different angle. He helps us by letting us see what seeing people's faith meant to Jesus. From Paul's letters, it emerges clearly that faith is the work of the Holy Spirit who gives it to us as a gift (1 Cor 12:9), as well as it being a work of God (Phil 1:29).[4] This

---

4. "To you it is given, not only to believe . . ."

makes it clear: the faith of the men bearing him and the paralytic himself drew Jesus' attention because he saw the work of God his Father and of the Holy Spirit. It follows that when the men came, Jesus saw in their faith the work of his Father and the Holy Spirit. Jesus sees God at work in the heart of those who come to him with faith. As he says himself in John's gospel, "No one can come to me unless the Father draws them" (6:44). With this, I can understand Jesus' emotion when, seeing their faith, he suddenly exclaims as he speaks to the paralytic, "My child." What emotion there is in this. It is a little as though Jesus was saying: Welcome, my child, you who my Father, in his grace, has led to me by faith, you in whom dwells the Holy Spirit who has given you faith. You are blessed, my child, for the faith my Father and the Holy Spirit have given you!

I also understand better why Mark held back from giving Jesus' name, only to state it at the moment it resonates with the mystery of the Trinity: the Son saw the work of the Father and the Holy Spirit in the arrival of the paralytic. What a profound mystery!

I also understand why Mark pauses his narrative to leave time to contemplate Jesus in his divinity. The pause is made by adding an untranslatable Greek particle (*dé*) at the beginning of the following verse to change direction (2:6). In order to mark this suspension of the story, I too pause at verse 6. The Son receives a sick man led to him by the Father and dwelt in by the Holy Spirit. "Jesus, seeing their faith, said to the paralytic: 'My child . . .!'"

"My child"

I am most surprised to see that Mark makes no effort to depict the paralyzed man. He doesn't give us his name, though he does so with Bartimaeus (10:46) and with Simon of Cyrene (15:21). He leaves our paralytic anonymous with no details at all, while with others he is much more forthcoming: he tells us that the woman with the hemorrhage had been suffering for 12 years and that she had spent everything hopelessly on visits to multiple doctors (5:25–26); he describes at length the Gadarene demoniac (5:2–5). I believe that he leaves the paralytic in obscurity to incite us to identify more personally with the text. We, who are also more or less paralyzed in our souls, in our spirits, in our faith, in our emotions and in our body; we who are to a greater or lesser degree dependent on the faith of those around us, we should not hesitate to draw near to Jesus, even if he seems beyond reach because of the crowd, even if we have no words to express our faith to him, even if we don't really know too clearly whether we believe in him or in God, and even if we are not sure God is at work in our lives or that the Holy Spirit is enabling us to believe. We must allow ourselves to be led by those who are bringing us to Jesus, even if this seems as crazy as being let down through the roof of a house, stretched out on a mattress! We must realize only that the Christ is there to receive us in an extraordinary way and with a magnificent word, "My child!" What a blessing to be welcomed like this by Jesus!

"My child": the form of address is frequent in the Septuagint (the Greek translation of the Old Testament used at the time of the New Testament). It's most commonly found, naturally, on the lips of a father speaking to his own child, as Abraham speaking to Isaac (Gen 22:7), and Isaac to Jacob (Gen 27:18). But also when a spiritual father speaks to his son, as does Eli to Samuel (1 Sam 3:16). We understand very well Jesus addressing his disciples in this way, calling them "my children" (Mark 10:24) as their spiritual father. Here though, with the paralytic, the situation is different: for Jesus, the man was an unknown, not one who would become a disciple and so stay with him. No, he would return to his home at the close of the account. So what was going on? Why does Jesus address him like this if he was not his spiritual father?

"My child": in this simple vocative there is a very evident love, a deep love, a love which the paralytic man surely cannot have expected, and he maintains a complete silence, unable to respond at all. It was a love that sprang from the depths of Jesus' heart, full of affection and tenderness: "My child!" How much greater is the shock of this when we consider with Mark that Jesus is God; the love is a divine love, issuing from deep in the heart of God! The profound silence of the man echoes the depth of the love that receives him.

Jesus had never seen the paralytic before; for him he was an unknown, one of the multitude of unknowns who gathered around him to see him and listen to him. The man had yet to open his mouth; he hadn't so much as addressed a prayer to Jesus, nothing to say why he had come, but Jesus had seen his faith, given him by the Father and by the Holy Spirit, and that was enough. Then we find Jesus welcoming him in the most lovely way, "My child." Mark doesn't attempt to describe Jesus' feelings when he saw the sick man's faith since Jesus' heart is unfathomable and indescribable, just like the heart of God. Nevertheless, there is so much love in these first words spoken by Jesus, the first he addresses to this unknown: "My child," as though the paralytic was amazingly close to him!

Jesus never again speaks like this to anyone in our gospel. We can understand him saying to his disciples "my children" (10:24) since they were not unknown to him; during the time they accompanied him, a real affection had grown. We can understand Jesus saying *talitha*, "little girl" (5:41) to Jairus' daughter of just 12 years; her age clearly admits of this. But this is not the case with the paralytic. The only other like case, which is just as surprising, is the woman with the hemorrhage who Jesus receives by calling her "my daughter" (5:34). It certainly wasn't Jesus' custom to receive strangers in this way.

Luke was undoubtedly surprised by the welcome Jesus reserved for the paralytic; he suppresses this "My child," replacing it with the much less affectionate and, as it seems to me, even cold, "Man" (5:20).

Before taking this further, it's important to ask if the paralytic was indeed an adult; might he not have in fact been a child? Why not? If that was the case there would be no surprise. The question might be asked, but I believe one detail in the account settles the matter: Mark carefully tells us that the paralytic was "carried by four men." If he was a child, two would have been enough to carry the bed. That there were four of them means he was an adult. The surprise that Jesus should call him a child therefore remains.

"My child": the love Jesus evinces is a paternal love, which is not to say that Jesus was in the place of a father to the man, but that the paternal love of Jesus is the same love he received from his Father, and he thus witnesses to the love he transmits from his Father. By speaking to the paralytic like this, Jesus was in no way taking the place of God; no, he was simply effacing himself before God as humbly as possible in order to reveal him. "Whoever has seen me has seen the Father," Jesus would say (John 14:9). Whoever hears me say "my child," is hearing my Father. Mark was writing to Christians who knew that Jesus never mistook himself for his Father, never substituted himself for his Father, but on the contrary, with his whole being was at pains to efface himself before his Father in order to reveal him. They knew that in response to this "my child," no one ever called Jesus, "my Father." The Christians Mark was addressing had been taught by Paul, indeed well taught, that the Holy Spirit witnesses in us that we are children of God the Father, and that is only to him that we say, "*Abba*, Father" (Rom 8:15; Gal 4:6).

In the heart of God

I believe we can investigate the way Jesus speaks to the paralytic a little further.

Nowhere in the Bible does God address anyone as "my child," while it is clear that we are his children: according to Paul, "We are children of God" (Rom 8:16). Why has God never spoken in this way? I believe that his reserve holds him back. God is so modest in his love that he never makes such an emotional statement. That God could be so moved shouldn't surprise us, not now that we are well into Mark's gospel, since from the opening of his gospel he points us in this direction, discreetly, with respect for God's modesty. He reveals strong emotion in God in his account of Jesus' baptism when God speaks to Jesus from heaven saying, "You are my beloved son" (1:11). Indeed, God was so moved, Mark tells us, that heaven "was rent open" (*schizô*). This splitting of heaven signals that God was moved to the core of his being.

This is God's nature. He was deeply moved when he said to Jesus, "You are my son," and so never said to him directly, not, at least, with human witnesses, "My son" or "My child," which would be more emotive still. Jesus must have heard such words in the intimacy of relationship with the Father; he must have heard this form of address and responded in like fashion, "*Abba*, which is to say, 'Dad'!"

11

14:36), and this would have been full of emotion for him too. None of the four gospels reports God saying to Jesus, "My child," but we can only suppose it to have been so when we hear Jesus replying with *"Abba."* We should respect the wonderful divine modesty in the intimacy of the Father and the Son. Nevertheless, Jesus was perhaps discreetly raising the veil on this a little.

In saying "my child" to the paralytic, I believe Jesus reveals the "my child" that God our Father restrains himself from saying to each of us, modest and reserved as he is. Jesus alone can reveal such a thing to us since he is God. He reveals it, and in the same way the Holy Spirit reveals to us that we can speak to the Father calling him *"Abba"* (Rom 8:15; Gal 4:6). If we can call the Father *abba* it must because hidden in the modest heart of our Father there is this "my child" which it would overwhelm us to hear, just as it is too much for him to state his love for us. Praise Christ for revealing to us so discreetly the modest, reserved love the Father has for us.

Just as in his divinity Jesus saw the faith in the heart of the paralytic, he also saw the infinite love in the heart of the Father. To see the invisible faith of the paralytic, and more still the unseen love of the Father for us, must surely belong to his divinity.

"My child": on hearing this, the paralytic ventured no reply. No doubt he had not expected such a welcome; and no doubt he was overwhelmed by such love. In fact, he remains silent to the end. There was good reason for him to be so radically affected, good reason to remain silent, contemplating the one who would speak to him in such a way . . .

"Your sins are forgiven"

"Your sins are forgiven": what a further new surprise it is to hear Jesus say this to the paralytic; certainly it is for us as readers since Mark has mentioned nothing about the man's sins. Nothing tells us that the man was a sinner. Would it mean the man's diseased state was a result of his sins? That is certainly possible, with the condition that we not generalize since not every paralysis is necessarily the consequence of sins. It might be the case, but not in a systematic way. In fact, faced with another disability, Jesus sought to separate sin and the sickness (John 9:2). A sick person is not a greater sinner than someone in good health; there is nothing to say that this paralytic was particularly a sinner. Nevertheless, Jesus announces to him the forgiveness of his sins. What a surprise! The man must have been expecting that Jesus would deal with his illness rather than with his sins. Jesus, however, saw fit to proceed differently.

Is it the case that Jesus would have wished to deal firstly with the more serious matter? That sickness would be less serious than sins? But it would be offensive to tell this man that his sickness was less serious than his sins. The opposite is also possible: would Jesus perhaps begin with the less serious matter? No. John Chrysostom was correct to think that the issue here has not to do with what was more serious, but rather that there was a question of humility. Jesus raises humility as an issue by intervening at the unseen level rather than the seen. The paralysis was visible to everyone, but sins are not, just as forgiveness is not visible. It was in order to avoid the grip of pride or vainglory that Jesus begins by announcing to the man before the whole world that his sins were forgiven. There is nothing in this that could draw the attention of others, nothing to arouse vainglory. Very humbly, Jesus takes his place in that which is invisible to the eyes of men. Already, by saying "my child," Jesus was safe from vainglory since this too belongs to the unseen: no one could see that the paralytic was a child of Jesus or of God. To say "your sins are forgiven" is also completely unseen since no one can see forgiveness any more than they can see sins. In the same way that Jesus deposits the invisible love of God into the sick man's heart, so he deposits the unseen forgiveness into the same heart too. There is nothing to impress the eyes of others.

Humbly, as always, Jesus effaces himself again but without saying expressly by whom the man's sins are forgiven. "Your sins are forgiven": the expression with its passive verb is imprecise, along the lines of the classic divine passive of Israel. To avoid pronouncing the name of God, Jesus says not "God forgives your sins," but "Your sins are forgiven." This was a classic practice in Israel and everyone understood it. Such divine passives are frequent on Jesus' lips as they were with those Jews who carefully avoided sullying the most holy name of God with their unclean lips. Thus, in the Beatitudes, when Jesus says, "Happy are those who weep for they shall be comforted," this means "they shall be comforted by God." It seems clear that when Jesus tells the paralytic that his sins are forgiven, he is giving him to understand that they are forgiven by God. At all events, the divine passive was perfectly understood by the scribes, who reacted immediately, as Mark informs us.

The scribes' reaction

The scribes did indeed react immediately; they were offended, but without giving outward expression to their thoughts. The reaction was internal. "They reasoned in their hearts," Mark tells us. However, just as Jesus sees the invisible in the heart, he also hears the inaudible, what is said in the heart. Here again a trait of his divinity is apparent.

"Why do you have such reasoning in your hearts?" Jesus says to them. The scribes were unmasked, but with plenty of delicacy. Jesus knew that they were accusing him of blasphemy but he doesn't uncover their accusation before the crowd. He spares them rather finely, but they knew that Jesus had understood what was in their hearts. What was going on in this quasi dialogue between Jesus and the scribes in which they hadn't even opened their mouths? We, in any case, need to understand how they could be accusing Jesus of blasphemy.

According to all we find in the Old Testament, no one could announce God's forgiveness apart from those God himself had charged to do so. It is similar at the merely human level: no one can forgive in someone else's place. How much more true this must be when it comes to God: who could be allowed to say that God forgives other than God alone? How could Jesus presume to tell the paralytic that his sins were forgiven? The scribes' reaction was perfectly justified; they had good reason to be offended. Who was Jesus to speak as he did?

Who, in fact, in Israel was authorized to say that God pardons sins committed against him? Properly speaking, nobody; and yet in his kindness and humility, God did charge certain men with announcing his forgiveness; the prophets and priests were authorized and they alone.

Thus it was that one day the prophet Nathan was sent by God to David to announce his forgiveness. If Nathan was permitted to say to David, "The Lord has forgiven your sin" (2 Sam 12:13), it was because God had charged him to do so, and this is specified at the beginning of the passage: "The Lord sent Nathan to David" (12:1). In the narrative,

Nathan uses formulae that belong to prophetic discourse like "thus says the Lord" (12:7). The same happens with the other prophets. Now the scribes would have noted, correctly, that Jesus was not a prophet in that he had not used the phraseology of prophetic discourse, not here or anywhere else in the gospel. Indeed, Jesus never used expressions such as "thus says the Lord, "in the name of the Lord, I say to you," or perhaps, "the oracle of the Lord."

As well as the prophets, priests were also authorized to proclaim God's forgiveness, and this would be following the rites of expiation, most often in expiatory sacrifices (Lev 4:40, 26, 31,35 . . .) But here, there is nothing of any of these rituals, and more, the scribes knew very well that Jesus was not a priest, not born of a priestly family. Therefore, he could not announce God's forgiveness.

The scribes were right; apart from the prophets and the priests, no one other than God could announce the forgiveness of sins. Who then was Jesus to speak as he had? Either he was blaspheming or he was God. Jesus made sure not to say before the scribes, "I am God"; never, because of his reserve and humility. They would immediately have cried out blasphemy, just as the high priest in fact did when, before the Sanhedrin, Jesus said, "I am the Son of the Blessed" (14:62). By replying, "I am," Jesus was saying something only God could say, as at the burning bush, when he appeared to Moses (Exod 3:14). By saying, "I am," Jesus was saying, "I am the one who is," which is to say, more than just the Messiah; it came down to saying that he was God. The high priest then denounced the blasphemy.

That day before the Sanhedrin, it was the eve of Jesus' death and he had nothing further to lose; he knew he was going to die, and the hour had come for him to state his divinity. But here, with the paralytic, it was not yet time. He was content to let the truth of his divinity be implied. He really is God and can therefore forgive sins, but it was not yet time to state his identity clearly.

"The Son of Man"

In order not to reveal his divinity, Jesus evidences great teaching skills as well as humility by putting forward the figure of the Son of Man behind which he could hide, identifying himself with this figure. He says, "The Son of Man has authority to forgive sins" (2:10). Saying this, Jesus must have upset the scribes again because they would never have heard anything like it; and, in fact, Jesus was saying something completely new here.

The Son of Man is an enigmatic personage, spoken of in just one Old Testament text (Dan 7:13–14). I will add the whole text here because we will be referring to it often: "I saw in the visions of the night, and behold with the clouds of heaven there came one like a son of man. He came to the Ancient of days (which is to say, God), and he was brought into his presence. And he was given sovereignty, glory and royalty; and all the peoples, nations and those of every tongue serve him. His sovereignty is an eternal sovereignty which will not pass away, and his royalty a royalty which will never be destroyed." This heavenly personage is so close to God that he could almost be God. This however was not something that could be envisaged at Daniel's time or by Daniel himself, and there was therefore nothing more he could say about his vision. The mystery of God is too great, too unfathomable. Only Jesus could add to it.

In the rest of the Old Testament the expression "son of man" is often found, designating a non-particularized person; it's often used to address Ezekiel (2:1, 3, 6, 8 . . .). But "a son of man" and "the Son of Man" are not the same. In the book of Daniel, there appears in heaven a being whom Daniel describes with nothing beyond the imprecision, "like a son of man." But, again, "like a son of man" and "the Son of Man" are not the same. However, after Daniel's time, in the inter-testamentary period, in particular in the books of Enoch and Esdras 4, the celestial figure of Daniel's vision so impressed itself on the thinking that he became "the Son of Man." This is how Jesus, always based on the Daniel's vision, comes to speak of the Son of Man.

In his vision, Daniel learns that God has given authority to the Son of Man, but without supplying anything more precise about the authority. It is Jesus who provides the precision: "He has authority to forgive sins." But who then was Jesus to be in a position to provide this precision? All Jesus allows to be understood here is that he is this Son of Man; it's not until later that he will let the meaning be clearly understood, in particular when he speaks of his death and resurrection: "the Son of Man will be handed over to the high priests and scribes; they will condemn him to death and deliver him to the gentiles; they will mock him, spit on him, flog him and kill him, and three days later he will rise" (10:33–34). It is he himself that Jesus describes in this way; nevertheless, here in chapter 2, this is only suggested, not stated clearly. We know that the scribes didn't react but were silent; we don't know if they understood that Jesus considered himself to be the Son of Man.

"God alone forgives"

As the scribes quite rightly thought, only God is able to truly forgive sins, and this is because his way of forgiving is beyond understanding. In Hebrew, there are many ways to speak about forgiveness, many verbs and expressions, but we will look at just two of them. In particular, there is the verb *nâsâ*, which means both to "forgive" and to "bear" or "carry." The verb can have as its subject both God and a person, and it signifies that the one who pardons takes upon him or herself the faults they pardon; they bear them in place of the person who offended, thus discharging them of the offence. This is the way God "forgives" (as in Gen 1:26; Exod 34:7) or a person forgives (Gen 50:17; 1 Sam 15:25).

Amongst the other verbs for forgive, there is one, *sâlah*, which has the peculiarity of having God as its only subject. The verb is used some forty times, but never to say that a person forgives. Only God forgives in this manner; people cannot. No doubt it was with this verb in mind that the scribes said that only God can forgive, so we need to ask what manner of forgiving this is that pertains only to God. How is his forgiveness different to ours? There is nothing in the verb itself or its derivatives which will help us specify the characteristic nature of divine pardon. Undoubtedly the pardon must be total, much deeper than ours but in a way that passes our understanding, and because there is nothing in the word *sâlah* itself which enables more precision, there is nothing to add. You would have to be God to know how God forgives, or perhaps you would have to be inspired by God; however, I think this inspiration, from God, is to be found in the Septuagint.

In the Hebrew text of Jeremiah, speaking about the new covenant, God uses the word *sâlah*, saying, "I will pardon their iniquity and will no longer remember their sin" (31:34). We discover here that the divine forgiveness is closely tied to God not remembering the sins he has forgiven. However nothing says that the forgiveness is synonymous with the not remembering. Not remembering might simply be a complement to forgiving: I will forgive, and moreover will no longer remember. The Septuagint translation is perfectly faithful to what the Hebrew says. However in the next use of the verb *sâlah*, the Hebrew text again reads, "I will forgive all their iniquities" (Jer 33:8). But here, very oddly, the Septuagint doesn't translate the Hebrew with the Greek equivalent, but replaces it with "I will not remember their iniquities." Amazing! The Septuagint translators, by substituting "not remembering" for "forgiving," make them synonyms, so this comes to saying that when God forgives, he no longer remembers the sins he pardons. You would have to be inspired to say this, and we thus find revealed by the Septuagint the particularity of God's forgiveness: he no longer remembers the sins he pardons. This is wonderful. God is certainly alone in forgiving like this because when a person forgives, we don't forget the offence we are forgiving, and this makes the forgiveness fragile. God is alone in forgetting the faults he pardons. What good news this is for each of us! Reader friend, all the faults you confess to God and which he forgives — he forgets. This is really liberating. You can know that he will never recall the faults he has forgiven you of because they have been scrubbed from his memory. You can know that on the last day he is not going to enumerate all the faults you have already confessed to him. God forgets the faults which we confess to him and which he forgives, and this makes his forgiveness of inestimable worth. Praise his name!

This magnificent prophecy of Jeremiah's is that much more important because it is taken up and used in the New Testament (Heb 8:12 quotes Jer 31:34 and Heb 10:17 quotes Jer 33:8).

"My child, your sins are forgiven," Jesus says. The paralytic had good reason to be overwhelmed because he was receiving from Jesus this divine forgiveness, receiving it from the heart of Jesus, who was also saying to him at the same time with so much love, "My child." The Father's love forgives and doesn't remember what he has forgiven his child of. If the man was paralyzed by his faults, laid out on his mat under the weight of his sin, then he was already healed in the depths of his being.

It's also the case that elsewhere God says he will not forget our faults (Jer 14:10: Hos 8:13), but there the issue is faults that have not been confessed to him. There is a magnificent invitation here to repent.

Heart repentance

One point, I believe, requires to be examined further, which is that the man had not asked for forgiveness. This is certainly the case, but more, he hadn't asked for healing either. In fact he didn't ask for anything; he didn't open his mouth, either before or after his forgiveness and healing. He certainly didn't say anything, but he believed, and Jesus saw his faith. No doubt he came with a real thirst for healing, and doubtless, it seems to me, with a certain thirst for forgiveness too, and this thirst must also have been part of the faith that Jesus saw. Seeing the man's faith, Jesus surely also saw his sins, but above all he understood the repentance in his heart. In the same way he heard the evil thoughts in the hearts of the scribes, he heard the repentant thoughts in the heart of the paralytic. How could the man's heart have been so full of repentance?

When the paralytic found himself before Jesus, his thirst for forgiveness could only grow. As Abba Matoès rightly said in the 4th century, "The closer a person draws to God, the more they see themselves as a sinner. In fact, the prophet Isaiah, when he saw God, declared himself wretched and unclean (Is 6:5)" (Apophthegm 514). This is perfectly true: when the prophet came into the Temple, we can be sure that he had followed all the rules for purification necessary to enter the sanctuary. Then, once he had come in and was standing before God, ritually clean, he laments his impurity. The light of God is like the sunlight coming into a room; the more light, the more evident are the spots and dust. We see this with Peter: when he saw the extraordinary catch he had just made, he cried out, "Depart from me, Lord, I am a sinful man" (Lk 5:8). Just before the miracle, Peter spoke to Jesus calling him "master" (5:5); and just after, he calls him "Lord," falling on his knees before this lordship. When he discovered the holiness of Jesus, if not his divinity, Peter also discovered the degree to which he was a sinner.

Further, what the paralytic knew of Jesus before presenting himself to him is only what he had heard; and what he had heard was that Jesus was speaking to everyone calling everyone to repent throughout Galilee: "The time is fulfilled and the kingdom of God is at hand; repent and believe the gospel" (1:15). We can validly suppose that if the paralytic was taken to Jesus, it must have been with a concern to move towards repentance. It's this that leads me to say that when Jesus saw the paralytic's faith he saw the faith of a penitent. The paralytic did not confess his sins out loud, but Jesus perceived the repentance in his heart, and that was enough. This is why he said, "My child, your sins are forgiven." It was with the same love and tenderness that he said "my child" that he announced his forgiveness. While the scribes believed there was blasphemy, the paralytic believed in the forgiveness of his sins. He believed with such assurance that he stood up when Jesus told him to do so. Thenceforth, nothing would hold him to his bed.

"I say to you"

When Jesus said to the paralytic: "Rise, take up your bed and go to your home" (2:11), he introduced what he was saying with the words, "I say to you." We will pause over this expression.

"I say to you": it is astonishing to see here that Jesus doesn't invoke anyone's name to tell the paralytic to stand up. Peter would later say to a sick man, "In the name of Jesus Christ of Nazareth, rise up and walk" (Acts 3:6); he would likewise say that the forgiveness of sins should be received "in the name of Jesus" (Acts 10:43). Paul would do the same as Peter and so say to an evil spirit, "In the name of Jesus Christ, come out of this woman" (Acts 16:18). The difference between Peter and Paul on one hand and Jesus on the other is huge. Peter and Paul relied on the authority of another, Jesus, to bring about a miracle or to announce the forgiveness of sins. In contrast, Jesus relied on no one to forgive or to perform a miracle, having the authority himself. He is "the Son of Man who has authority to forgive sins," just as he had authority to call upon the paralytic to stand up. He has the authority as the Son who has received the authority of his Father at the heart of the Trinity.

In Mark's gospel, Jesus never either performs a miracle or speaks "in the name of God" as did the prophets. Jesus is more than a prophet. His "I say to you" spoken to the paralytic has the authority and power of a divine word. The power of the Word of God means that what it announces is accomplished, as at creation: "God said 'Light be,' and the light was" (Gen 1:3). That is what is happening here: Jesus says to the paralytic, "Stand up," and he stands. The prophet Isaiah reports a word of God that makes this very clear: "As the rain and the snow come down from heaven and do not return without having watered the earth and caused the plants to grow, or without providing seed to the sower, so is my word that goes out of my mouth: it shall not return to me without effect, without having executed my will and accomplished my plans" (Is 55:10–11). "I say to you" has the power of a divine word since the Jesus who spoke it is not a prophet who transmits and speaks in the name of God, but is God speaking on his own divine authority.

"I say to you": this is great discretion on Mark's part. He reports these few words without any commentary, it is enough to reveal Jesus as God.

In the gospels of Matthew and Luke, we find the same as here in Mark, that Jesus does nothing in the name of God or in the name of his Father. Everything he does is on his own authority, his divine authority. It would seem to be not quite the same in John, but only in appearance; it is more nuanced but the result is the same.

In John's gospel, then, Jesus says this: "I do the works in the name of my Father" (10:25), which seems to put him on the same level as the prophets. But we should not be mistaken; his speaking in this way is a matter of humility, to honor his Father, because elsewhere he speaks quite differently, in fact that the Father acts in the name of the Son: "The Father will send the Holy Spirit in my name" (14:26). This last verse is surprising: we see God the Father, who does nothing in anyone else's name, acting in the name of Jesus, his only Son. How wonderful this is: the Father is so humble that he acts in the name of the Son, just as the Son in his humility acts in the name of the Father. Neither of them is a prophet to the other; each is as humble as the other; each defers humbly to the authority of the other.

Here in Mark's gospel, Christ's humility is manifest differently, not in his leaning on the authority of his Father

24

but in effacing himself behind the figure of the Son of Man who has received authority from his Father: "That you may know that the Son of Man has authority to forgive sins, I say to you, Stand up, take up your bed and go to your home."

"Stand up"

"Stand up," Jesus says; the paralytic "stood," Mark continues, so here we have the miracle: "Stand up, arise . . . and he stood." Mark says nothing further about the miracle itself but simply leaves us to contemplate this event beyond our understanding . . . It is enough for us to contemplate and marvel . . . "He speaks and it is" (Ps 33:9).

Mark says nothing more, but what he does say deserves some attention. His Greek is not entirely covered by our translations, and we need to note a disconnect of sorts between Jesus' command to the paralytic and its realization. Jesus says, "Arise!" What happens when Mark describes the command's fulfilment? Our translations are a little off target. Properly speaking, Mark says not "he rose up," but more precisely, "he was raised" (ègerthè). The verb Mark uses is not in the active or middle voice but is passive.

The use of the passive signifies clearly that the paralytic didn't get up on his own but that someone helped him rise. Who could it have been that raised him? Mark doesn't say, not wishing to use the name of God superfluously. However it's quite clear: the passive verb is very definitely a divine passive, which gives us to understand that it was God who caused the man to arise. Who else, indeed, could have done this? The miracle is there; God had stepped in, causing the paralyzed man to arise.

God certainly acted, but in a most discreet way. He stepped in without accompanying his intervention with the slightest sign of his presence, with extreme humility. Here the wonderful humility of God is evident. The paralytic found himself on his feet, without Mark giving us any detail that would help us understand how the man was raised. God stepped in with a total effacement of self, no doubt so that the crowd would attribute the miracle not to him but to Jesus.

"We have never seen anything like it": saying this, the whole crowd "glorified God," as Mark specifies. The crowd glorified God, but to whom did they attribute the miracle? To Jesus or to God? "They all glorified God": who was meant here by "God," God the Son or God the Father?

In the account of the raising of Jairus' daughter, Jesus accompanies his words with an action: "He took her by the hand and said, 'Little girl, rise up'" (5:41). The passage continues, "The little girl arose," here with an active verb not passive, showing that it was Jesus who performed the miracle. Again, in the account of the healing of the possessed boy, Jesus performs the miracle without a word, [5] just with a simple action: "Taking him by the hand, he lifted him up," and, Mark continues, "he stood up" (9:27). There is no divine passive here, underlining that the miracle is to be attributed to Jesus. The situation here is very similar, but there is no action from Jesus; he simply speaks, as indeed is emphasized: "I say to you, arise." This "I say to you," really emphasizes the power in Jesus' word. It is therefore he who did the miracle by the power of his word, but there is no action from him, as though he didn't want to push himself forward but, as humbly as possible, leave the accomplishment of the miracle to his Father. The divine passive is there to indicate that, yes, the Father stepped in.

5. Jesus does speak (v 25) before this, but not to the boy; he addresses the spirit.

What shall we say further? On one hand, the Father intervenes as discreetly as possible to give place to the Son; and on the other, the Son's intervention is as discreet as possible to give place to the Father. In this we see both the magnificent humility of the Father and the equally magnificent humility of the Son, his divine humility. The humble Son is truly in the image of his Father.

In the end, then, who brought about the miracle? I believe that Mark would have us understand that the Father and the Son accomplished it together, that the Father and the Son worked together in perfect harmony, without either of them being more prominent than the other, each humbly self-effacing before the other. It's certainly the case that what one desires, the other desires equally; Father and Son have one will. Their union is one of absolute perfection, beyond anything we can say. It's so inexpressible that Mark contents himself with writing, "He was raised," without naming who did the miracle, leaving unspoken the perfect synergy of the Father and the Son. Then he concludes by saying that "all glorified God," without specifying exactly who is meant by the word "God," leaving us to contemplate Jesus in his insoluble bond with his Father, beyond anything that can be said. "Who sees me sees the Father," Jesus says elsewhere (John 14:9).

Just the same is true of the forgiveness extended to the paralytic. Jesus said to him, "Your sins are forgiven," again with a divine passive, letting us know clearly that it was the Father who forgave him. "Your sins are forgiven," means that they were forgiven by God the Father. The scribes reacted to this by accusing Jesus of blaspheming since they understood Jesus to be attributing to himself the right to forgive. They were mistaken in accusing him of blasphemy, but they were right to think that Jesus was presuming to forgive the paralytic's sins. The conclusion emerges from this that it belongs to the Father to forgive, but also to the Son, who "has authority on earth to forgive sins." When Jesus says, "your sins are forgiven," the sub-text is that they are forgiven by both the Father and the Son; both forgive in communal agreement, with communal mercy, in perfect harmony. The divine passive allows room for them both.

The Father and the Son forgive in just the same way as the paralytic's healing pertains to both. I believe that in this passage, Mark the contemplative invites us to contemplate the Father and the Son in their profound communion and in perfect synergy, as much in the gift of forgiveness as in the healing. "All that the Father does, the Son does likewise" (Jn 5:19); similarly, "I am in the Father and the Father is in me" (14:11), and "I and the Father are one" (10:30).

"Take up your bed," and "he took up his bed"

"Take up your bed," and "He took up his bed": the verb here, translated as "take up," is active on each occasion; there is nothing of the passive here. The paralytic man alone took up his bed in obedience to Jesus' command. He took up his bed, and this was a visible sign to him of the great event that had taken place in his life. The bed would be a memorial to keep as evidence that the Lord God, Father and Son, had magnificently intervened in his life.

This is the first time the man had carried his bed. Until this point, his friends had carried both the bed and him on it. Henceforth, he would carry it on his own. He could leave by the door, having entered by the roof. No longer were there sins in his heart, and he had his bed on his shoulders; and this was much lighter! In his heart he had God's forgiveness, filling him with thanksgiving. He was not carrying his cross; he was carrying what had been his cross.

We could say that he was as one resurrected.[6] "He was raised up," we read, just as we read concerning Jesus on Easter morning (16:6, with the same Greek word, ègerthè).

"Go to your home," and "He walked out before them all"

"Go to your house": by saying this, Jesus refers the man back to when he called him, "my child."[7] He has no desire to hold on to the man and make him his disciple. He doesn't seek to monopolize him; his love is not possessive; no, it's a disinterested love which humbly discounts itself in favor of family.

We should recall that Jesus similarly referred to his disciples as "my children," but he didn't tell them to go home, instead keeping them close to himself. His love is not possessive, but neither is it distant; always he has it just right, knowing what to say that is best for each of us.

The paralytic says nothing, no more than did the disciples the day they were called (1:16–20). They all obeyed Jesus' words. Jesus was alone in speaking, and his word forms, shapes, fashions those who obey him.

"We've never seen anything like it"

In fact there is more than just one miracle in this passage, there are two: the miracle of the forgiveness of sins and the miracle of the healing, the first invisible to the human eye, and the second plain to all; both are relayed to us with a divine passive ("your sins are forgiven" and "he was raised"). The two divine passives speak of the indescribable communal activity of the Father and the Son.

6. The French here is *ressuscité*, which obviously translates directly into English as *resuscitated*; it is often used in French for *resurrected*.

7. Giving him a very simple instruction.

Is the miracle of the forgiveness of sins genuinely invisible? Not entirely. At all events, the fruit of the miracle can't escape our eyes; the face of a person who has been forgiven is not what it was before; transformed by the divine forgiveness, it lets an inner light which comes from God be seen.

Everyone there could see the paralytic pick up his bed, and they could also see him forgiven with his face shining; they all cried out, as Mark tells us, "We have never seen anything like it."

"We have never seen anything like it": at the point Mark gives us this final exclamation, the paralyzed man had already left. "He walked out before them all," we are told just previously. The man had therefore left, but Jesus was still there in front of the crowd, so everyone's eyes would have been fixed on him, contemplating him. Mark ends his account here, silent to contemplate and leave us too to contemplate Jesus in the infinite mystery of his humble divinity, in the image of his humble Father.

How blessed we are to contemplate the Son who humbly effaces himself behind the Father who forgives and heals, and thus we contemplate too the Father humbly effacing himself behind the Son — who forgives and heals.

Lord Jesus,
the paralytic has left, and you are here in front of me.
I bless you, you who see in my heart what I cannot see myself,
who see in my heart the hidden work of the Father
who, in his grace, has enabled me to believe in you;
you, who see in my heart the discreet work of the Holy Spirit
who impels me to turn to you in prayer.
I have no words to tell you what I feel,
but you see the passion of my soul athirst for you.
I bless you, you who see the child I am in your Father's heart
and the measureless love the Father has for me.
I bless you, who welcome me with tenderness
in my thirst to meet you.
Before I tell you the faults within me,
before I find words to leave them in your heart,
before even I open my mouth,
you have forestalled my clumsy repentance
and given me your pardon and the pardon of the Father,
that infinite pardon that wipes away from your heart and
 the Father's
all we have deposited there in repentance.

O Lord Jesus, I bless you
because your deep love and divine forgiveness
have relieved me already of my despondency,
my inner blockages and discouragements,
from everything that ties me down and paralyzes.
On my feet now, I stand before you and gaze upon you,
my heart full of thanksgiving and wonderment.
Lord Jesus, grant me to stay a little longer before you,
to contemplate you in the infinite beauty of your deep
 communion with the Father,

*so that I can live henceforth in newness of life among
my brothers,
I pray, you who live and reign with the Father and the
Holy Spirit
now and always through endless ages. Amen*

THE DEMONIAC

(Mark 5:1–20)

1. They arrived at the other side of the sea, in the country of the Gadarenes. 2. Immediately he had left the boat, there came to meet him from among the tombs a man with an unclean spirit. 3. He had lived in the tombs and no one could bind him, not even with a chain; 4. he had often been placed in shackles and chains but had broken the chains and burst the shackles; no one was able to master him. 5. Night and day, he was among the tombs and in the mountains, crying out and cutting himself with stones. 6. Seeing Jesus from afar, he came running and fell down before him. 7. After crying out with a loud voice, he said: "What have you to do with me, Jesus, Son of God Most High; I adjure you by God not to torment me." 8. This because he had said to him, "Come out of the man you unclean spirit." 9. He asked him, "What is your name?" and he replied, "My name is Legion, because we are many," and begged him insistently not to send him out of that country. 11. Nearby, on a hill, there was a great herd of pigs that were feeding. 12. They begged him, saying, "Send us into the pigs, let us enter them." 13. He gave permission, and the unclean spirits came out, entered into the pigs, and the whole herd rushed to throw themselves off a cliff into the sea, about two thousand of them; and they drowned. 14. The men who were in charge of the pigs fled and told what had happened in the town and in the countryside; and the people came out to see. 15. When they came to Jesus and saw the demoniac seated, clothed and in his right mind, the very man who had had the legion, they were overcome by fear. 16. The eye witnesses explained in detail what had happened to the demoniac and the pigs, 17. and the people began to pray Jesus to leave their district. 18. Then, as he was getting into the boat, the man who had been demonized prayed that he might stay with him. 19. He did not authorize him to do this, but said to him, "Go to your home, to your own people, and tell them what the Lord has done for you, and how he has had pity on you." 20. He went and began to preach in Decapolis what Jesus had done for him, and they were all amazed.

THIS TOOK PLACE ON FOREIGN TERRITORY, BEYOND THE SEA of Galilee, in Gadara, one of the cities of the Decapolis. Jesus had crossed the sea to come to this gentile area. When he was getting out of the boat, there came a man can running to him, a man he would heal. At the close of the account, when Jesus gets back into the boat, the man is now speaking with him. The mention of the boat at the beginning (v 2) and the end (v18) of the passage points us to the discovery that Jesus came to the Gadarenes for this encounter alone. He arrives just before and leaves immediately after; this tells us how important the encounter must have been to him.

If it had just been an unforeseen episode in a wider project, Jesus would have stayed in Decapolis to accomplish that project. There is nothing of that. Immediately after this one event, Jesus returned to Galilee. His object had therefore been accomplished; the goal of his trip had been to encounter this man and heal him.

When still in Galilee, before getting into the boat to make this trip, Jesus had told the disciples, "We are going over to the other side" (4:35). This order, given without any explanation, gives us to understand that Jesus was determined on the excursion, that he had a very precise project in mind, but one that he did not reveal to his disciples. The disciples were to be part of the expedition and be present at the encounter, but without knowing why. This all leads us to think that Jesus had to meet this Gadarene.

It follows that Jesus made this return crossing just for him, which is very wonderful when we consider that this man, this gentile,[8] was seriously unwell. Jesus crossed the sea solely for him, this unknown! He even had to endure a severe storm for him alone, as Mark tells us in his account of the crossing itself, making it a day out of considerable turbulence (4:35–41).

That Jesus should make this trip to Decapolis for one afflicted person indicates a great interest if not love on Jesus' part. To show the value of this man to Jesus, Mark reveals simply that it was greater than the value of a herd of two thousand pigs, which is enormous. It's wonderful to see that a simple stranger, a deeply unwell man, profoundly deranged in his spirit, should be of such price in Jesus' eyes.

8. In French, *païen*; meaning both gentile and pagan.

What could there have been so important about this gentile, this sick man, that Jesus would invest so much time and make so much effort to deliver him from his hell? He had simply this, that he was a man, a creature formed by the hands of God; this is why he was of such price to Jesus. In the end, reader friend, he is like each of us, we beings who are loved by God; for each of us, Jesus became a man; for each of us he goes through the storm of hell to snatch us from the grasp of the evil one. Our text is wonderful about this: it demonstrates the price each of us has in the Lord's eyes.

"A man in an unclean spirit"

What was the man suffering from? Mark tells us that he was a demoniac but without using the word "demon." He prefers a synonym and speaks of an "unclean[9] spirit." He does this using a most surprising phrase, telling us that the man was "in an unclean spirit." When it's translated to say that he was "possessed by an unclean spirit," this is not wrong; the meaning is not incorrect, but the phrase still merits our attention.

"A man in an unclean spirit," Mark tells us: whatever the translation, this doesn't mean the spirit of the man was unclean. It was clear to Mark as it was to Jesus that the unclean spirit needed to be dissociated from the man. There were two separate beings, quite distinct from each other. If we find it difficult to believe in the reality of unclean spirits or demons, we have to acknowledge that Mark believed and that Jesus did too, unless we completely overlook what the text says. The way the Bible speaks about unclean spirits may repel us, but there is no good reason for this. If

9. The French throughout is *impur*.

I understand it properly, I believe we can say that unclean spirits, that is evil spirits as Luke terms them (7:21; 8:2), designates the spirits which generate wrong thoughts within us. Evil, wrong thoughts don't spring up spontaneously; they are brought by evil spirits, and we might add that this somewhat lifts the burden of guilt. What are evil thoughts? All the thoughts which sully our relationship with God and with others; not only lustful thoughts, but thoughts of pride, vainglory, anger, jealousy, all the spiritual maladies that the Church Fathers termed the passions, which pervert our life with God and with others. Having said this, we can now delve into the text just as it is.

"A man in an unclean spirit": word for word this is interesting in that shortly after, Jesus challenges the unclean sprit, saying to it, "Unclean spirit, come out of this man" (5:8). That it had to come out clearly means that the spirit was "in" the man. So what are we to understand? We find that the man was "in" the unclean spirit, and the unclean spirit was "in" the man. We need to understand that there was a very deep link between the man and the unclean spirit.

This deep link has in the Fathers the name "perichoresis"; this describes a relationship of interpenetration between the two, one in the other and reciprocally. I hesitate to use the term here because the normal quality of perichoresis is a love relationship. It is a wonderful word which speaks of love beyond any other love; it is the word to designate the inexpressible love among the three Persons of the Trinity. When Jesus says, "I am in the Father and the Father is in me" (John 14:10), perichoresis expresses the relationship of infinite love within the Trinity. It is also a wonderful gift Jesus gives to us as he invites us to abide in him and he in us (John 15:5), drawing us and integrating us into the love of the Trinity. Here, the relationship between the unclean spirit and the Gadarene is anything but one of love; it's no more than an imitation, a sad, crude imitation of love. So, saying this, I would comment that what the unclean spirit had established with the man was a caricature of perichoresis.

For Jesus, that there should be such a bond between a man and an unclean spirit was extremely serious. It was even simply blasphemous since, for him, such a bond should exist only with God; the apostle John states this clearly in his letter, speaking of a Christian believer: "God abides in him and he in God" (1 John 4:15). In Jesus' view, the one and only real perichoresis for a person must be with God, whether with the Father, with the Holy Spirit , or with him, the Son.

Here, however, the Gadarene man was in an unclean spirit and the unclean spirit was in him. I understand now why Jesus made the voyage to the Gadarene country in order to meet this man. The man's situation was extremely serious, even blasphemous. The unclean spirit was occupying in this man the place that belongs only to God. It's so serious because through this unclean spirit, the Evil One, Satan, was at work, his one project being to occupy a place properly belonging only to God. The whole Bible shows us that this is Satan's objective, and that unhappily he often succeeds in filling this place in a person's heart. Jesus' reaction is immediately comprehensible.

"We shall go over to the other side," Jesus had been Jesus' determination to the disciples, without explaining something they would have been hard pushed to understand. He wished at all costs to fulfil his purpose, to the point of enduring a severe storm. The moment he arrived in the Gadarene area, immediately, with his first words, Jesus spoke to the unclean spirit, telling him uncompromisingly and with the greatest authority, "Come out of the man, unclean spirit!" (5:8)

The whole gospel shows us how important it was to Jesus to dislodge Satan from the place he abusively held in people's hearts. In fact, this passage is an illustration of a major theological theme; it describes through a detailed example an issue that concerns humanity as a whole, whether Israel, the people of God, or in Decapolis among pagan people. It's wonderful that we can embrace this passage, discovering in what is an extreme example, something that concerns in varying degrees every person on earth, each of us personally.

When it comes to us, evil thoughts suggested by evil spirits often do no more than pass through us without any further action because we reject them. Sometimes though, they stay and meet with our assent; then they can become installed and end up enslaving us. We are then "possessed" by them and need to be delivered. Today we no longer speak of possession but of addiction, but this comes to the same thing, to slavery. Thus there is addiction to anger, pride or jealousy, just as there can be addictions to cigarettes, alcohol, or to television or the internet. Our spirit is then invaded and to a greater or lesser extent we are upset in our relations with others and with God.

"Come out of the man!"

Before going further into the passage, I would like to pause over these words addressed by Jesus to the unclean spirit: "Come out of this man." If we translate the expression like this, it is not exactly wrong, but it does slightly abuse the text. Word for word, Jesus didn't use a demonstrative, just the definite article: "Come out of the man." It's true that in Greek the definite article at origin was a demonstrative and at times retained that sense, as here; nevertheless, it did have the full meaning of simply a definite article, "Come out of the man." What Jesus is saying is very important because what he was saying with respect to this Gadarene, he says on behalf of people in general, for everyone, for every person, for each of us: "Come out of the man, unclean spirit!" Wonderful! We see here the importance of these words which are to be understood at the level of humankind. "Come out of the man, unclean spirit!" That is, "Come out of every person, unclean spirit!" Jesus came to earth to say this. The stakes are very high; high enough that Jesus would cross the sea and endure a storm to say it.

Who was Jesus to throw himself into such a confrontation with Satan? Definitely, defying such an adversary in such a way must be because he is God. It requires God's authority to say "unclean spirit, come out of the man!" In a similar account, Paul said, "In the name of Jesus Christ" (Acts 16:18), but here Jesus speaks on his own authority; in this, he is God.

"A man"

We return now to our Gadarene man, without forgetting the theological stakes we have just examined. This man was in a profoundly bad way, more than can be readily believed; spiritually he was seriously sick. However serious his condition, it is no less true that the sick man was still a man, fully human, and it is this that we need to hear when Jesus speaks. "Unclean spirit, come out of this man": Jesus doesn't say "come out of this diseased body," or "come out of this gentile unbeliever," but "come out of this man." However sick, a man or a woman remains exactly that, a man or a woman in the eyes of the Lord. It was to save a man that Jesus crossed the sea; it was out of love for him that he endured the storm.

Mark understood very well what was at stake in Jesus' actions. In fact the first word chosen by Mark in speaking of the Gadarene is "man." He tells us: "Immediately Jesus got out of the boat, there came to meet him *a man*" (5:2). Certainly this was a man "in an unclean spirit," but above all, it was a man. The rest of the account depicts his state of ruin, but this doesn't mean we're not dealing with a man who remains fundamentally a man. He lived among the tombs and was on a highway to death, but was still nonetheless a man. In this passage, Mark uses a very strong verb, saying that no one was able to "master" or "tame" him (5:4). This man may have seemed no better than a savage beast, but that makes him no less a man.

This word "man" is the same given in Genesis to Adam. The Gadarene was a man created in the image of God (Gen 1:26). Even in his piteous condition, in total ruin, the Gadarene was a man in the image of God. It was to meet this man that Jesus traversed the sea in order to return his human status to him, to restore in him the image of God. What love! The love of Jesus doing so much for him is the love of God for his human creature, for each of us, created and fashioned by God himself in his image and likeness. Will we ever know how much we are loved by God, loved by Jesus? We discover a little of it here when we see what took place between Jesus and this Gadarene, living like a beast, isolated and abandoned by all, living among the tombs and inhabited abusively by, I would say, this "squatter," this unclean spirit; in fact by an entire legion of unclean spirits! I say "squatter" because the true possessor of the human heart is God. In infinite love, Jesus crosses the sea for him and sovereignly intervenes to such an extent that he was to be found "seated, clothed and in his right mind" (5:15). These three adjectives are the high point of the passage; they describe the man as he might have been pictured in the garden of Eden: seated, clothed and in his right mind. This is humanity in the image of God.

Hell among the tombs

What can this man's life have been before Jesus came? The detailed description Mark gives us clearly gives us to understand that it was a living hell. He had established himself in a cemetery, in the place of the dead. No one really wished him ill, but he took it upon himself to self-harm, Mark telling us that, "he cut himself with stones" (5:5). No one spoke to him and he spoke to no one. In fact he no longer spoke; instead he cried and shouted, with Mark saying, "He was crying out among the tombs and in the mountains" (5:5). The use of the verb "cry" in the participle form describes time without end, a present that never stopped. "Night and day," Mark specifies. In short, the man's life was an eternal hell: "Night and day, he was crying out and cutting himself with stones among the tombs and in the mountains."

"Crying in the mountains"

The man's cries, similar to the cries of a wild animal, dramatic as they were, nevertheless had an extraordinarily positive aspect; I would even say miraculous. What am I saying? There is nothing surprising about his crying among the sepulchers, not in the hellish context; it just shows the stranglehold the unclean spirit had over him. The man was totally subdued by it, bullied, and dehumanized to the point he had nothing but cries to yell among the tombs, where no one could reply to or even understand what he said. This was a real hell! But the amazing thing is that he cried out "in the mountains." This is both amazing and wonderful. Throughout the ancient Middle East, among the gentiles as well as in Israel, the mountains were not the domain of demons but were holy places, the home of the gods. Demons or unclean spirits lived in the tombs or the deserts, but not in the mountains. In Revelation, we see a demonic beast rise up out of the sea (13:1) and another from the earth (13:11), but not descending from the mountains; this is not their domain. In Babylon, where there were no mountains, the people built artificial mountains, the ziggurats, in order to provide the gods places to live, holy places; likewise in Greece there was Mount Olympus which was the home of the gods; and the mountains of Zion, Carmel and Sinai were holy mountains where God had made his dwelling.

So we see this demoniac crying in the mountains, not once, not from time to time, occasionally, but all the time, "night and day" as Mark specifies. This is really out of the ordinary: "Day and night he was crying in the mountains." Yes, he was also crying out among the sepulchers in his submission to the unclean spirit and cutting himself with stones in the grip of the unclean spirit, but that was not all he did; he was also crying out in the mountains as though to escape the demons' grip. This means that the man was both a slave and a free man.

One detail from the account shows that the man was indeed going into the mountains in an attempt to turn to God; this detail appears in the words of the unclean spirit to Jesus when he challenges him, terming him "the Son of God Most High." "The Most High": this is the only time God is called this in Mark's gospel. This way of speaking of God was well known to the gentile pagans; it's a term used in the Old Testament: "I will ascend above the clouds; I will be like the Most High," said a Babylonian king full of pride (Is 14:14). If God is the Most High, it makes perfect sense to go into the mountains to call upon him.

Who is there powerful enough to lead this man into the mountains and so escape the grip of an unclean spirit, even of a whole legion of unclean spirits? I can only see one answer and it takes on a special savor when we remember the way Mark had been influenced by the apostle Paul.

"The Holy Spirit cries out in our hearts"

The only one who can stand against an unclean spirit is the Holy Spirit. No doubt this is why Mark speaks of an unclean spirit rather than a demon, so as to make a contrast between the two spirits. The only spirit able to lead the Gadarene into the mountains to meet God is the Spirit of God. The unclean spirit cannot resist the Holy Spirit. What was the Holy Spirit doing after leading the man to the mountains? He was there in the cries, turning them Godwards; he was crying out in the man's cries. Paul has two illuminating comments here, saying both that our prayers can be a crying out in the Holy Spirit (Rom 8:15), and that these cries are the cries of the Holy Spirit in our hearts (Gal 4:6). Even if the cries of the Gadarene were no more than the cries of a beast, it's no less true that the Holy Spirit himself was crying out through them, turning them into prayer. What was the nature of this prayer according to Paul? It's extraordinary: *"Abba,"* a prayer addressed to God the Father (Rom 8:15; Gal 4:6).

The Gadarene "was crying out in the mountains," Mark tells us, formed in his thinking as he was by Paul. Wonderful! Thanks to the Holy Spirit, our Gadarene was able to escape the hold of the unclean spirit and pray in the mountains, even praying "night and day," which is to say without ceasing, just as Paul calls us to do (1 Thess 5:17), and as did Jesus himself (Luke 18:1).

We have here a beautiful teaching on prayer: the unclean spirit, even an entire legion of unclean spirits, was able to possess a man but was unable to prevent prayer to God because the Holy Spirit was always there to lead him in prayer. Even the most severely affected people are always capable of praying. The cruelest tyrants can't prevent anyone praying, and we see this in the most anti-religious totalitarian regimes. Nothing can prevent a person from praying, even if the prayer resembles the cry of a wild beast, and if it's no more than a groan, a moan or even mute. The Gadarene was crying out in the mountains and his cries were prayers launched towards God. What a miracle!

I had the opportunity to baptize an autistic man who could only emit incomprehensible sounds; I was never able to reach him or to establish eye contact with him, but in the end I one day understood that in his inarticulate words there were prayers. I understood this on the day of his baptism; he had let me lay my hand on his head to baptize him and his eyes met mine; I then saw deep in his eyes the light of God . . .

We can thus understand that the Gadarene, despite the hold of the unclean spirit, was able to pierce the sky with cries to God there in the mountains through the grace of the Holy Spirit, and that in his cries which were incomprehensible to men, God heard the Holy Spirit cry out, *"Abba."* Satan can mislead a person, but that doesn't mean that they are not in the image of God and always capable of prayer thanks to the Holy Spirit praying within.

The blessed perichoresis

When Paul talks about the prayer addressed to the Father, *"Abba,"* he says on one hand that the Holy Spirit cries out *in* our hearts (Gal 4:6) and on the other that we cry out *in* the Holy Spirit (Rom 8:15). Paul is pointing to a real and wonderful perichoresis between the Holy Spirit and ourselves. If an unclean spirit interposes and shuts us into a caricature of perichoresis, it can only do so as a squatter; it can't prevent the true proprietor, the Holy Spirit, from remaining with us in the true perichoresis, the primary perichoresis initiated by God with us from eternity. It's good to know this.

If the divine perichoresis is primary, we can ask if the Holy Spirit continues to live in the same place as an unclean spirit. There's a very pertinent remark by Philoxene of Mabbug (of the 6th century): "Does a doctor leave his patient when he finds him attacked by some disease, and then not return until his health is recovered? No! It's precisely when his patient is sick that the doctor sits assiduously at his bedside."(Cited by Sebastian Brock: *Prière et vie spirituelle,* Bellefontaine 90, p.160.) The love of God is so great that he never stops working by the Holy Spirit in the heart of his children, even those most overrun and cruelly misled by the Adversary.

The same applies to both this picture of the true perichoresis and its caricature, as in the parable of the good wheat and the tares (Matt 13:24–30). The field God sows with good seed is God's field and will always be so even if the Adversary comes along and sows tares. A person is always in the image of God even if a legion of demons comes to squat in his or her heart. We may be slaves to our passions, prisoners of pride, jealousy, lust or a whole legion of demons, but the Holy Spirit will always be our true proprietor, at home in our hearts, in perichoresis with us, deep down inside us, sovereignly there to lead us in prayer along a pathway of freedom leading to the full freedom procured by Christ.

It is Christ's mission to set us free, and that's what we discover here in what he does for the Gadarene. Jesus crosses the forbidding sea, we might even say the infernal sea, and comes to command the unclean spirit with sovereign authority, "Unclean spirit, come out of this man!" (5:8), and the remainder of the account tells us clearly that not only did the spirit come out, but more specifically, as Mark tells us, "The unclean spirits came out" (5:13); that is, the entire legion of unclean spirits came out. Then, as a wondering Mark continues, the man was found to be "seated, clothed and in his right mind" (5:15). Mark invites us to contemplate this man healed, set free by Jesus, sovereignly healed by "the Son of God most high." I marvel each time I read this verse that celebrates the work of Jesus: "He who had had the legion was seated, clothed and in his right mind."

"He who had had the legion": how wonderfully well said. The grip of the demons was gone, finished. There was total freedom, and as Mark tells us just before, the legion of demons sank into the sea, a little like Pharaoh and his whole army, lying dead at the bottom of the Red Sea the night of Passover (Exod 14:27–28).

I never fail to wonder at this text, and might well end my comments here, but there are a few further enlightening points to consider.

The Father listens

It's clear to me that God had heard the cries of the Gadarene. The whole Bible tells us so very clearly: when anyone cries to God, he hears. "The Lord heard when I cried to him," the psalmist says (Ps 4:4). "I cried to God and from his temple[10] he heard my voice; my cry came before him, into his ears" (Ps 18:6). Many other texts go in the same direction.

The Gadarene fled into the mountains to cry, and his cries must have been just like the cries of wild beasts; but that doesn't matter because God perceived his prayers through these cries; he could not do otherwise as we understand since the Holy Spirt was crying through him. He was crying, *"Abba,"* and the Father heard. Even if the demoniac was unaware of the presence of the Holy Spirit within him, that's by the way; God knew and he heard. This is a great thing to know, and it's the same for every person, for every seriously afflicted pagan unbeliever: God hears the cries we raise to him.

When Hagar, a pagan Egyptian, was cast out by Abraham, she fled into the desert with her child and sat down to weep; God heard the voice of the child and sent an angel to save them (Gen 21:17).

Whether in the mountains, in a desert, or wherever, God hears; we see this with Jonah, who cried out from the depths of his own private hell and then burst out in praise, saying to God, "From the place of the dead, from its depths, I cried and you heard my voice" (Jonah 2:3). If Jonah was heard from the place of the dead, then I believe the Gadarene was heard by God, not only as he cried among the mountains but also as he cried among the tombs. There is no need to go to some holy place; it's enough just to pray, even from a morgue, a concentration camp, a prison or any other place of suffering; God hears and answers.

10. Fr. *palais*, palace.

The Father sends the Son

When Israel was enslaved in Egypt, no prayer is reported in the Bible at any point during the period. However, in the account of Moses at the burning bush, God says: "The cries of Israel have reached me . . . And now, go, I am sending you to Pharaoh" (Exod 3:9–10). God had heard their cries and sent a liberator.

What was going on with the Gadarene? I believe that the Holy Spirit impelled him to cry out, that God heard his cries and that he sent his Son to free him from his distress. This is why Jesus said to his disciples, "We are going over to the other side!" but without telling them that he had to cross the sea to set the Gadarene free from his hell. I am unable to understand Jesus' profound desire to go the country of the Gadarenes any other way; it was to meet this one man, this sick man, to free him from the oppression of the unclean spirit. I believe that this was the mission he had received from his Father. Jesus didn't explain his mission to the disciples, and neither does Mark make it explicit, though the little he says and gives us to understand seems to me to become clear in the light of the rest of his gospel and Paul's teaching. Emerging from all this is that the Holy Spirit led the sick man into the mountain to the Most High, and that the Most High sent his Son to deliver him. Again, it becomes clear in the light of the Trinity, humbly hidden away in our passage: the Holy Spirit cries, the Father hears and sends his Son to save the man. What depth there is to this text!

We mustn't forget that what Jesus does here for the Gadarene is what he does for all of humanity, for each of us. The Holy Spirit prays in our hearts, the Father hears and sends his Son to save us.

"He ran"

Equally clear to me is another aspect of this wonderful account. Mark tells us that the Gadarene, "Having seen Jesus from afar, ran and fell down before him" (5:6). This is really astonishing! Why did this man set out at a run towards Jesus? Was he behaving like this towards everyone who was there? Was he throwing himself headlong from the tombs to frighten and attack them? I don't know, but that wasn't his attitude towards Jesus: he ran to Jesus, not to attack him but to fall down before him. This prostration had nothing aggressive about it; rather, it was a cry for help. He ran up to the person from whom he expected his freedom. He fell down in the way one falls down before God. That he was behaving like this when he didn't know Jesus says to me that the Holy Spirit was at work in his heart. Just as he had led him towards the Father in the mountains, he led him to run to the Son to fall down in an attitude of supplication.

The unclean spirit speaks

The following part of the account does, however, pose a problem. If we want to understand the passage, we need to recognize that the demoniac was being impelled by both the Holy Spirit and the unclean spirit. Both were at work in him, one for his well-being, the other to hurt. It's true! And this is why, when the man fell on his face before Jesus, it wasn't the Holy Spirit bringing him to speech but the unclean spirit who spoke, even preventing the Gaderene himself from speaking. The speech Mark records clearly shows that it was not the man speaking but the unclean spirit speaking through him: "What have you got to do with me, Jesus, Son of God Most High; I adjure you by God not to torment me!" It was the spirit speaking, not the

Gadarene, who was so beaten down by the unclean spirit that he was unable to speak himself. In fact, the Gadarene didn't speak until the point of his being set free. He was prevented from speaking; only the spirit did so.

Mark had already set us up for this in a preceding passage concerning the incident in the Capernaum synagogue: "A man who had an unclean spirit cried out, "What have you to do with us, Jesus of Nazareth? You have come to destroy us. I know who you are, the Holy One of God" (1: 23–24).

The situation is very similar. "The man cried out," Mark tells us, but the words that follow were not the man's but the unclean spirit speaking in him. However, Jesus wasn't mistaken about who was speaking, as the continuation shows: "Jesus rebuked him, saying: Be quiet and come out of this man (1:24–25). Who was Jesus rebuking? Not the man but the unclean spirit. What happened next? Mark tells us that "the unclean spirit came out of the man" (1:26). The man in the Capernaum synagogue didn't utter a word; the unclean spirit had stolen the man's speech and spoke in his place.

It's important for us to know this, even when we are not demoniacs ourselves. When we are in the grip of some passion such as anger, for example, we need to know that we are not giving expression to ourselves but that the anger is speaking through us, even if, as here, we are speaking to Jesus. Often our prayer is not our own but comes from the passion inhabiting us, whether it be anger, pride, jealousy, vainglory or whatever other. The passion within us, even momentarily, speaks and prays through us.

Pay attention! If we examine our prayers carefully, we will note that from time to time, happily not always, it's not really we who pray but this or that passion that grips us.

When we note this, we should not be discouraged. Run to the Lord and bow down before him; he will know what to do and will take care of us.

With the Gadarene, the same happens; it is not he who is speaking but the unclean spirit, and Jesus understood this very well. As we read the passage closely, it's made difficult by the way Mark inverts the order of the speeches. He reports the words of the unclean spirit (v 6) first and then the words of Jesus (v 8), when the actual order was the reverse, as the verb tenses indicate: "Crying out with a loud voice, he says (present), 'What is there . . . ?' (v 6), because "Jesus had said (past), 'Come out of the man . . .'" (v 8). Mark proceeds like this to show how pervasive was the stranglehold of the unclean spirit over the Gadarene.

What we see is the Gadarene in a forced submission to the demon; he no longer had the right to speech. He prostrates himself before Jesus, but is unable to even get his prayer out; the unclean spirit had robbed him of speech and was speaking instead of him, telling Jesus of his fear: "Don't torment me." It was not the Gadarene who was afraid of being tormented but the unclean spirit who knew very well who Jesus was, the Son of the Most High who had come to command him to leave. The unclean spirit then sought to negotiate the terms of his exit, asking to find refuge in the herd of pigs.

The Gadarene came running to Jesus, fell down before him but said nothing, silent. Wonderfully, though, Jesus understood his silence; he understood that he was shut in to a silence imposed by the unclean spirit, imprisoned in silence. Jesus had come to set him free and to free him into speech. First, he began by dialoguing with the unclean spirit; he then imposed a definite silence on it culminating in the drowning of the pigs at the bottom of the sea, thus setting free the Gadarene, who suddenly found himself freed from his imprisonment, "seated, clothed and in his right mind."

Two silent men

Once set free, what did the Gadarene do next? He didn't immediately speak, but now this was of his own volition. To begin with, he was silent, and Mark says nothing further since events were beyond description. The Gadarene was seated, clothed and in his right mind, in silence before his liberator, who was silent too. We are invited to consider these two men in the silence, sharing the silence beyond words; each contemplated the other. The Gadarene was unaware that Jesus had crossed the sea just for him, that he had braved a storm before finding him, the lost sheep. Never would the Gadarene be able to measure the depth of Jesus' love for him. He knew nothing of all this, but he did know he had been set free; he kept silent, contemplating his deliverer. None of us will ever be able to measure the depth of Jesus' love for us, but we can be silent before him, contemplating the one who has crossed the darkness of death to set us free.

As for Jesus, I believe that he was contemplating in this man, as he does in each of us, a person who had been created in the image of God who had now recovered his full humanity. "He who had had the legion seated, clothed and in his right mind."

How long did Jesus and the Gadarene spend together without a word? If we look closely at the account, we see that they remained so long enough for the men who looked after the pigs to spread the news "in the town and the surrounding country" (5:14). Throughout this time, Jesus and the Gadarene stayed together in silence, a blessed time of great peace and wonderment. Reader friend, let us too take time to sit down alongside them for the time the pig keepers were away! We do well to pay attention to the pauses we find in the gospel accounts; they are open doors to contemplation. The guardians of the pigs are away spreading the news to all around, and we suspend our reading and rest alongside Jesus and the Gadarene, in silence as we await the arrival of the locals. Let's not move on too quickly; we can take our time to contemplate . . .

"They come to Jesus and see the demoniac"

Mark continues his account like this: "They came out to see what had happened; and so they come to Jesus and see[11] the demoniac seated, clothed and in his right mind" (5: 14–15). Who is the "they" here? Mark doesn't specify, but we understand it to have been the local population. If Mark was vague, I believe it to have been a discreet way of including us among the local people, so let us be led along in this same way . . .

"They came out to see (*oraô*, v 14) . . . and to contemplate (*théôréô*, v 15)": Mark uses two different Greek verbs here which unhappily are usually translated by just one verb, "see." What a shame! The change from "see" to "contemplate" indicates that as we look at the Gadarene the way we see changes, passing from the surface to the depths, from the visible to the invisible. The Gadarene was not the same anymore; he was no longer the formidable and uncontrollable demoniac but a man "seated, clothed and in his right mind." What had happened? The verb for "contemplate" (*théôréô*) means that something coming from God ((*théos*) had taken place, that God had intervened and had something to do with the great change. We

11. The French here means "contemplate": see the next paragraph, which also covers the use of the present tense.

therefore contemplate the work of God in this man's life. Mark invites us to spend time in contemplation; he does so by changing tense: he uses the past in "they came out to see" (v 14) and the present in "so they come to Jesus and gaze" (v 15). Mark has us move on from the past to wonderfully open before us a present without limits, a present that can be eternal . . .

What is it we can "contemplate"? And what might those who came have seen? Well, they saw what was invisible to human sight, invisible in the way that God is invisible and beyond words. Until this point the unclean spirit had been master of the Gadarene, but that was no longer the case. God had stepped in; but how? The Gadarene was saying nothing; he was silent; he contemplated Jesus; who can say what was going on? Our eyes now turn naturally to Jesus; he too is silent; he is contemplating the Gadarene. Is there a connection between God and Jesus? The people from the surrounding area didn't know Jesus; they looked on, dumbstruck! Mark lets us contemplate all this. Thanks to him we know more, much more than the local people about Jesus. Not only had Jesus intervened but so too had the Holy Spirit and God the Father. And so we contemplate: the three times holy God had stepped into the life of this man who was now seated, clothed and in his right mind . . .

Then, Mark continues: "They were seized with fear." This last verb is a wonderful conclusion. This fear is the fear we have before God, holy fear, a fear made up of immense respect that has nothing to do with frightened, cowering fear; it is the reverential fear which fills us when God lets himself be seen (contemplated) in his work. "To contemplate" and "to fear": these two verbs together focus on God. This holy fear stops us in our tracks in contemplation . . .

We therefore stop right here and remain in this contemplation. No one can forbid us, and Mark leaves us with all the time we need; than he continues his account.

An expert report

The resumption of the story is brutal (5:16–17), taking us at a jump from the depths of contemplation to simple surface reality. The people who now step into the picture are "those who saw," not "those who gazed," so this means the men who were looking after the pigs. We will not be surprised to learn that what they said had nothing in common with any contemplative witness.

"Those who saw exposed in detail": the verb chosen by Mark means "expose in detail." No doubt they came forward with lots of details, but which? The result of their statements was that Jesus was begged to leave the area, which he did without delay: he got back into the boat.

What was going on? Which details did they furnish that led to the request for Jesus to leave? Mark doesn't specify, but tells us enough that we can understand: "They set forth in detail what had happened to the demoniac and with respect to the pigs." It's clear. These people gave their expert opinion, not a testimony to the work of God. What God, Father, Son and Holy Spirit had done was not part of the discussion; it cannot be "exposed in detail." No, it's too deep, beyond telling. In contrast, it was much easier to give the details of the financial loss. They knew the value of the pigs as well as they knew their own pay. They knew how many pigs there were and how many workers. The pigs had disappeared into the sea and were beyond recovery, of no value; the men had lost their work and were now jobless. Expert opinion was therefore established with its logical conclusion: Jesus was responsible for the financial catastrophe and had to leave. Perhaps we should be glad that he wasn't expected to compensate the owners of the pigs or the workers!

They had detailed what had happened to the pigs, but what did they say about the demoniac? They spoke of him as though he was still the same demoniac, although that was over and gone. They couldn't speak of this correctly because they were incapable of saying how it was that he now seemed to be "seated, clothed and in his right mind." How could you give a detailed account of such a thing? Jesus had acted, but what exactly had he done? He had said nothing to the Gadarene and only conversed with an unclean spirit! How can you report in detail a conversation with an unclean spirit? It wasn't Jesus who had driven the pigs into the sea; it was the demons who had done that! But would it be believed that a legion of demons had entered the pigs and thrown both pigs and themselves into the sea? This is not a story you can readily tell!

How could you make clear that the cries of the demoniac in the mountains were, through the Holy Spirit, prayers; that the Most High God heard these prayers, and that he had sent his Son to deliver the demoniac? This is all beyond telling, just like the profound change at work in the heart of this man who was now seated, clothed and in his right mind.

In short, "those who saw" gave the details but not the depth of what had happened. There we have the whole difference between an expert report and the witness of a contemplative.

Also, why was the Gadarene himself not asked what had happened? It seems that nobody thought of this, though he was now well able to speak. However, no one even tried to find out if this was so. All that was known was that he had spent his time crying out, even at night, among the tombs and in the mountains, and that this had brought fear to the people. Now, though, he was crying no more. There he was, silent, seated, clothed and in his right mind, but no one called on him to speak. Perhaps his report would not be from the expert standpoint? Would he instead bear witness to what Jesus had done in his life? If he had been asked to speak, I believe Jesus would not have been asked to leave the country!

And what of Jesus, who thought to ask him? No one.

Then, Mark concludes, "They began to pray Jesus to leave their district" (5:17). He says this with a touch of humor. He chooses the verb "pray," to alert us to the fact that Jesus is the person to whom prayers are addressed, not one to whom expulsion orders are issued.

The Gadarene's prayer

In the final part of the account (5:18–20), Mark demonstrates a delicacy towards the Gadarene by not continuing to speak of him as a demoniac (in the present) but using a past tense to say that he had been a demoniac. It's very lovely: we see the man respected in his full humanity, in the image of God.

As Jesus was just about to get into the boat, the Gadarene addresses him in prayer. Again, it's lovely as finally we see him speaking. Until this point he had been prevented by the unclean spirit speaking in his place; then, after the healing, the local people hadn't given him any opportunity to speak and he couldn't have felt free to speak before them anyway, no doubt sensing their distrust or fear. We can understand: it had been so many years since anyone had spoken to him or asked him to speak to them. They had heard only cries that resembled the cries of wild beasts.

But with Jesus, the Gadarene felt sufficiently confident to speak up even before Jesus spoke to him. His first words were a prayer. It's wonderful to see that once he was free to speak, re-established in his humanity and the image of God, he began with prayer. This is the true image of God, with prayer the first communication.

What did the man ask in his prayer? He wanted to be with Jesus, that is, to stay alongside him, to climb into the boat with him among the disciples. This was his deep desire —to be a disciple. Nevertheless, humbly, he didn't wish to lay claim to being one; no, he asked Jesus; he prayed for his desire to be accepted.

"Go to your house, to your own people!"

Magnificent as the prayer was, this didn't prevent Jesus denying his request. The man's desire was not Jesus' desire for him. This is illuminating: Jesus does not always fulfill our prayers, great though they might be; his desire may be different to ours. His desire is not uniform: he asks some to be with him and to follow him, as he asked of the Twelve, but of others he may not ask this and even turn down a request, as with the Gadarene. However, this refusal is explained. Jesus had another desire for this man, another project, just as wonderful: not that the Gadarene be with him but that he be with his own people, in his own home. The missions Jesus gives us are diverse; callings are diverse and complementary. Jesus knew that the Gadarene still had plenty of love to give to his own and plenty of love to receive from them, love which had been blocked up for so long.

Jesus had said to the paralytic, "Go to your home" (2:11); to the demoniac he says a little more, "Go to your home, to your own people." Initially this addition seems redundant, a little superfluous, but, in fact, this really isn't so and just demonstrates a heightened attention on Jesus' part to each person's situation. The paralytic must simply have left his home that very morning; I have difficulty imagining his bearers carrying him several miles or for days. Having left the same morning, the paralytic would go back home and pick up the daily routine, certainly with a much easier life, but he wouldn't have been away for long. It was quite different with the demoniac, who had lived among the tombs for months or even years. Returning to his home meant going back to a place he had long since left. It was in taking account of this long separation that Jesus insisted, "Go to your home, to your own people." Jesus was re-establishing family ties broken years before, underlining that for the demoniac his family had not disappeared, that they were awaiting him, and that family are always family. We see that Jesus' instruction had a resonance much greater for the demoniac than for the paralytic. So, having said this, we see the close attention Jesus gave the demoniac! This finesse reveals that for Jesus the family is of great price. This can be important for us in our reflections on the family at a time when so many families are suffering.

"Go to your house, to your own people," Jesus tells him. "To your own": not to the unclean spirits who have laid their hands on you without the remotest touch of love for you but to your wife and children who love you and who you love. Love does not grasp another person to possess them but is a free gift of self. Go to your home, to your own. On the one hand, there are those who bound you with chains and shackled your feet; this is not love. Those bonds have broken you, but there are other bonds, bonds that have been broken, the bonds of love with your wife and your dearest. Go to your home; the bonds there are always alive. Go and revive them by going home. The place you have found to live in the tombs is not your real home; it's no substitute for your home, so go to your real home which is there with your loved ones, in their hearts. You have been gone so long. Go back to your own people.

As we see, reader friend, Jesus doesn't ask the same of everyone. Of some he asks that they leave wife and children, brothers and sisters; of others that they go back to their own.

The unclean spirits had established a control over the Gadarene, but Jesus did not wish to now do the same. His love was not possessive; he sent him back to his own. Once the Gadarene had returned to his home, the love of Jesus for him would remain, as we can suppose the love of the Gadarene for Jesus would remain.

"Tell them all that the Lord has done for you!"

Jesus' instruction to the Gadarene continues: "Go to your house, to your own people, and tell them all the Lord has done for you, and how he has had mercy on you." Go to your own and talk! It's so long since they have heard you speak. No doubt they heard your cries, which must have rent their hearts. The cemetery is not so far from the village; they must have heard you crying. Now, they need to hear you speak; it will be a balm to their hearts. Speak, but not about your hell, about the years of suffering. Don't dump your sack of pain on them. Tell them about the Lord, about God; not in the way a theologian would speak, abstractly and theoretically. No, tell them about God concretely; tell them what he has done for you. Don't tell them about the unknowable and ungraspable in his being, but about what he has done for you.

Jesus' request is clear; he asks the man for his personal testimony. But be careful, Jesus says, don't push yourself forward, talk about God. Don't say what you have done, what you have done for him, but what he has done for you; not what you have done for him previously, not what you will do later, but what he has done, for you personally. More precisely, "How he has had mercy on you." Don't talk in a general way about the pity of God, his mercy, about his grace; talk about his mercy on you, concretely. Then your people will understand that God is a God who has pity, which is to say that he feels deeply, that he is moved to the core,[12] that he even has mercy on a pagan gentile like yourself, a sick man like you, a man who had become a wild beast, a man prevented from speaking by a demon, a man able only to cry, a madman able to tear apart chains. Tell them all this so that they understand that the Most High God is able to come down very low, right into a man's private hell to deliver him. They have to understand because it's not something they know. The god they've heard about in Decapolis, in Gadara, is not the God who has cared for you; he's not the god of the Greeks who has no guts, no emotions. Tell them that the mercy of God is active, alive, not just a sentiment or feeling.

"He went and began to preach"

This was what Jesus asked of the man, and it is exactly what he set out to do, though not in quite the stated way. What follows in Mark is this: "He set out and began to preach in Decapolis all that Jesus had done for him." This is both very close and very different.

12. Fr. *Entrailles*. Translated below as "guts."

In accordance with the terms stated by Mark, the Gadarene did indeed tell just what had been done for him. He didn't launch into theological abstractions but stayed with the concrete facts of what had happened; he stuck to personal testimony.

However, there was a difference because he wasn't content to speak just to those close to him, in his house, but went to preach throughout the Decapolis. Perhaps he had understood "your own" to mean everyone in his country, of his nation. We can be indulgent; leaving behind the tombs and the hell of unclean spirits had made him an enthusiast. We see him set free, we might say, from a foreign legion and ready now for the conquest of the whole of his home land! We can well understand: his deliverance was magnificent.

One special feature that varies from the instruction is that he didn't speak about "the Lord" but about Jesus, and this is a most important difference. For Jesus, "the Lord" meant God, his Father, not himself. Jesus is too humble to call on the Gadarene to talk about him and what he had done in freeing him of the unclean spirit. If we look at Mark's gospel as a whole, we find that on each occasion someone wished to talk about Jesus, Jesus wanted him silent. It's a constant in the gospel. Every time, Jesus imposed silence (1:44; 7:36; 8:36). The Gadarene is the exception, the only one Jesus asked to speak. As the exception though, Jesus didn't ask him to speak about him, Jesus, but about "the Lord," his Father. This is indeed Jesus' humility, not wishing to speak of himself but of his Father.

I believe that for us as readers all this is evident; however, I believe that for the Gadarene things were not so clear. In fact, for him to speak of what God had done for him was *quasi* impossible because he didn't know what God had done for him. In his own country he had learned that God is "the Most High" (5:7); he had gone out into the mountains to cry to God Most High, but he didn't know if the Most High had heard him from on high. He had cried out day and night without receiving any indication of response. He did know that Jesus is "the Son of God Most High" and that this Son had stepped down out of a boat, setting his feet on solid ground — so while God is the Most High, his Son comes down very low.[13] He knew that he had thrown himself on the ground before this One who is most low and that then there was no need to cry out because this lowly One had delivered him from his torment and brought him out of his hell through his immense pity. So, if the Gadarene was to speak of the Lord and of his pity on him, the Lord might indeed be the Most High in his heaven far above the mountains, but it was above all the lowly One who had appeared to him. This he could tell; he could tell all that the Lord Jesus had done for him in his immense pity. And so, Mark tells us, the Gadarene preached throughout Decapolis all the Lord Jesus had done for him.

Mark no doubt delighted in writing this page of his gospel since for him too Jesus is the Lord, with this to add, that he is Lord just as is God his Father; and that Jesus is the lowly One come among men and women while also the Most High, seated in the heights at the right hand of the Father.

The Gadarene, then, went to preach in Decapolis, to preach, not just to tell in the way Jesus had sought of him. The use of the word "preach" is highly significant since it is the term that characterizes the mission of the apostles, just as Mark teaches at the beginning of his gospel: "Jesus appointed the Twelve to send them out to preach" (3:14).

---

13. The French might be best translated literally as the "Most Low."

We also learn in the book of the Acts that Peter went to preach in Caesarea (10:42), Philip in Samaria (8:5) and Paul at Damascus (9:20), at Ephesus (20:25) and at Rome (28:31). Acts teaches that the apostles went throughout the earth, but doesn't say anything about the Decapolis! Why? Because the preaching of the Gadarene was enough: he had been the apostle to Decapolis; his preaching had been blessed, so much so that there was no need to preach after him. As the Holy Spirit had been with him in the mountains in his cries, he was with him in Decapolis to preach.

The Gadarene wished to be a disciple, and in fact he became an apostle; in the grace of God, his apostleship bore fruit.

"All were astonished," Mark concludes. "All"; that is to say all who heard the Gadarene, all his family members, all his neighbors and no doubt all who had insisted that Jesus leave their land! As they heard the Gadarene's preaching, all understood that Jesus is truly the Son of the Most High.

O Holy Spirit, blessed are you who with such love
joined yourself night and day to this man in distress
eliding yourself into his cries and making them prayers.

O Father, blessed are you who with such love
heard the pleas of this man in distress
and sent your Son to draw him out of his hell.

O Jesus, blessed are you who with such love
delivered this man from his highway to death
and restored him to his family that grieved his loss.

O Holy Spirit, do not stop inhabiting our cries and making
*   them prayers;*
open up our prayers in the silence
as we contemplate Jesus our deliverer
before we step out to preach of all he has done for us.

O Father, cease not to hear our cries and our groans
and fill our hearts with your peace
as we contemplate your Son in silence beside you,
and then step out to preach of all he has done for us.

O Jesus, never stop visiting our hells to pull us from them;
keep us united to you in the silence
as we taste with you the beauty of closeness
and then step out to preach to the ends of our pagan world.
We pray this of you who live and reign with the Father and
*   Holy Spirit,*
now and always throughout the ages. Amen

THE MULTIPLICATION OF LOAVES

(MARK 6:30–44)

30. The apostles gathered around Jesus and told him all they had done and taught. 31. He said to them, "Come apart into a deserted place and rest a while;" so many people had been coming and going they had been left without so much as time to eat. 32. They left in a boat for a quiet place away from the crowd, 33. but they were seen leaving; many learnt of it and came running out of all the towns and reached their destination before them. 34. When Jesus got down out of the boat, he saw a great crowd and was moved with compassion for them because they were like sheep without a shepherd. He began to teach them many things. 35. When it was getting late, his disciples came to him and said, "This is an empty place and it's late. 36. Send the people away so they can go into the surrounding country and villages where they can buy something to eat." In reply he said to them, "You give them something to eat yourselves." They said, "Are we to go and buy two hundred denarii worth of bread and so feed them?" 38. He replied, "How many loaves of bread do you have? Go and see." After checking, they said, "Five, and two fish." 39. Then he commanded them to make everyone sit down in groups on the grass. 40. They spread out in groups of a hundred or of fifty. 41. He took the five loaves and the two fishes, and, lifting his eyes to heaven, he blessed and broke the loaves and gave them to the disciples to hand out to the people; and he shared the two fish among them. 42. Everyone ate and all were filled. 43. They gathered up twelve baskets full of leftovers with the fish; 44. and those who had eaten amounted to five thousand men.

THIS LENGTHY GOSPEL PASSAGE IS OF INTEREST TO ME FOR its account of the multiplication of the loaves, but it would be a shame to look only at this because it's an integrated passage, the unity of which we should respect. The multiplication of the loaves took place in a "deserted place" (6:35), but the place had been chosen by Jesus for another reason, to give the disciples a time of rest (6:32). The connection between the disciples' rest and the multiplication of the loaves has a meaning we need to grasp.

Reinforcing the connection between the two (the rest and the multiplication) is the boat, which we are told of firstly in verse 32 as the means of reaching the destination, and then again at the close of our passage (6:45). The essence of the account takes place between one embarkation, and another.

The unity of the whole passage is also due to the constant presence of the disciples alongside Jesus; they make up more than just the backdrop they had been in the accounts of the paralytic and the demoniac, but take an active part, firstly, with respect to their need for rest and then in the miracle of the loaves. As for the crowd, they were simply the beneficiaries, much less active than the disciples; it was not the crowd who asked for food but the disciples on their behalf.

Return from mission

At the outset of the account, before taking a rest and retreating into a quiet place, the disciples begin by regathering around Jesus (6:30). They are returning from a mission, which is why Mark calls them "apostles." An apostle is a person sent on a mission. They had scattered, without Jesus, sent by him to accomplish their mission (6:7–13); then they regrouped alongside him once their mission was finished, and they told him "all they had done and taught," recounting everything, not among themselves but to Jesus. In a sense we could say they were already conducting something of a retreat in that they were speaking only to Jesus and not to each other. They were speaking to Jesus, which is as much as to say they were praying, addressing Jesus alone on their return from mission. Jesus says nothing at the opening of this passage; the disciples monopolize speech. Jesus listens, and this too amounts to a retreat, a time when Jesus is totally open to hearing us, is "all ears," an attentive listening which is rare today.

"They recounted everything": Jesus didn't interrupt them. He gave them time to tell him all that had happened. This is great. Then, after they had had their full say, Jesus proposed that they have a time of rest "away from the crowd, in a deserted place." This is the beginning of a retreat as envisaged by Jesus, and he now took matters in hand because he wanted them to understand what a retreat was about; this was something they were yet to discover as it's likely they hadn't experienced it before. At this moment they had told Jesus everything they had to say, but just speaking to Jesus was not yet a real retreat, but only the preamble. This is often the case with us too. When we go on a retreat, we usually start with a time of prayer in which we tell Jesus everything; and this is good. Jesus, though, is waiting for us to have finished talking so that we can enter into the depths of a retreat with him.

Jesus on retreat

What constitutes a retreat for Jesus? It's something Jesus is described as experiencing in Mark's account at the beginning of his gospel, where we find the only other use of the phrase "a deserted place" (1:35). Jesus was now leading the disciples into a deserted place, one favorable to silence and solitude; it is here, in a deserted place, that he had previously been on retreat. Mark tells us in the briefest way of this, Jesus' retreat; to say more is to touch on the inexpressible. Here is what Mark tells us about Jesus: "Towards morning, while it was still very dark, he got up and went out into a deserted place; and there he prayed" (1:35).

"To go out into a deserted place" is exactly the expression that Mark uses again concerning the disciples with Jesus: "They went out into a deserted place" (6:32). This phrase is not found elsewhere in this gospel; clearly, Mark wished to link the two passages.

What did Jesus do while on retreat? "He prayed." Mark says nothing more; the rest is beyond words, belonging to the intimacy between Jesus and the one to whom he addressed his prayers, his Father. Mark tells us nothing further, not even the contents of Jesus' praying. This is Jesus' secret, his intimacy with his Father, an inexpressible intimacy.

The difference when it comes to the disciples is that the disciples' retreat was communal; "apart," "in a deserted place," certainly, but together. Perhaps Jesus intended to share with them what a personal, solitary retreat was to him? We don't know because any such plan was short circuited by the crowd. Certainly, though, Jesus was proposing a retreat to them all, communal and not personal, whereas according to 1:35, a retreat for Jesus meant this: being alone with the Father.

When Mark tells us that Jesus "prayed" in a deserted place, the Father is not named; I would further add that the Holy Spirit is not named either, and I believe we should include him too. When the Father and the Son share time together, it is also with the Holy Spirit, as we are told elsewhere: "Jesus thrilled with joy through the Holy Spirt and said, 'Father.'"(Luke 10:21). Mark says simply, "He prayed," without adding anything since he knew very well that Jesus' praying belongs to the mystery of the Trinity and is beyond expression. Mark's extreme sobriety demonstrates here his profound and discreet respect for the divine intimacy. It's enough for us to contemplate in silence.

When Jesus was on retreat, in 1:35, we learn that Peter came along and disturbed him! (1:36) Poor impulsive Peter, always a little too fast! He might have done better to ask Jesus to include him in the retreat — but no! Mark tells us of course that he didn't come out alone to seek Jesus but was with others (1:36), so it was actually impossible for Peter to be alone with Jesus even for a moment, and if he had been, it would surely have been very bold to ask of Jesus a place alongside him in his retreat. No one is really up to that, and that is as it should be: when Jesus prays, what else is there for us than prayer as well — in silence?

There is another difference to note between a retreat as experienced by Jesus and by ourselves. When Peter came out to seek him, Jesus told him that he had withdrawn to prepare himself for the next step in his ministry: "Let us go into the neighboring villages so that I can preach; this is why have come" (1:38). Clearly, for Jesus a retreat was a time of preparation for the rest of his activities, a time to look to the future not the past.

The disciples on retreat

We should note that Jesus did not propose a retreat to the disciples until after he had listened to them recount all they had done and taught. First of all, he listened. He didn't treat reflecting on the past lightly. This is important: we do well to take time on retreats to go over our past activities. However, we note that after waiting for them to finish discussing the past, Jesus turns the disciples to the future, along the lines of his own personal retreat. Jesus takes the remainder of his disciples' retreat in hand; he directs things. The crowd may have barged in unexpectedly, but Jesus manages the situation, which was to remain a retreat for the disciples. The rest of the passage demonstrates that this was so. The disciples' retreat in this deserted place would be wonderful, very profitable to them, an amazing overture to the future.

What did Jesus do? He welcomed the crowd and began to teach (6:34). The disciples were no longer speaking; they had had their turn, at length, and had said all they had to say. Now, in the deserted place, during this time of retreat, it is Jesus who speaks. He uses all his time to teach, there in the deserted place, in the place of retreat: "He began to teach many things," Mark specifies. He was addressing the crowd, but the disciples were not forbidden to listen!

That is the nature of a retreat: tell Jesus everything and then listen.

The disciples too had "taught" (6:30), and now it was Jesus who was "teaching" (6:34). Mark repeats the word: it was a wonderful occasion for the disciples to compare what Jesus taught with what they had taught. A retreat for the disciples was, as it is for us, a time to listen to Jesus and compare his teaching with our own, to correct it, to modify it and renew it; in short, to be taught by Jesus how to teach and to speak to others. I am sure that the disciples must have noticed the differences, and that it will be the same for us in our retreats when we put the gospel up against our preaching.

It strikes me in what the disciples said about all they had done and taught that they were at the center of it: "They recounted to Jesus all they had done and taught." That's fine, but what did they say about all God had done for them, with them and through them in their mission? They said nothing! As they listened to Jesus teach, no doubt they discovered how very present and at work in their mission God had been, much more than they had believed at the time. How often it is that only after the event do we discover, as we go over things, that God was present without our being aware of it. A retreat gives us time to examine our memories for the signs of God's presence in our daily lives.

They would also have discovered that Jesus teaches with "compassion" (6:34). We will come back to this, but right here we can ask ourselves about our teaching, witnessing and speaking to others: is it with compassion?

Before looking at the issue of compassion, we can pause over another moment in the disciples' retreat, the time spent with Jesus in the boat. Mark doesn't go into details, but it's a time we need to consider. The crossing of the sea took place with no sign of a storm; it was a time of perfect quiet in the sense that Jesus proposed: "Rest a little." Yes, they were going to rest as they listened to Jesus teach and be nourished by his teaching, but the crossing of the sea was restful too. It took place at such a gentle pace that the crowd overtook the boat. Mark tells us that the crowd came "running" (6:33), but a crowd that runs is still slow, especially if, along with the women, children and the elderly in the crowd, there were the sick, as stated by Matthew (14:14). At all events, the crowd hurried as best they could, fast enough to outstrip the boat.

What took place in the boat? Nothing, it would seem. But nothing when alone with Jesus is never nothing. No, it's beyond words. The disciples enjoyed a wonderful time of retreat; they said nothing, and neither did Jesus; they were there together in the boat and this was a part of their retreat, this time without and beyond words, beyond prayer, in Jesus' silence; a time in which the disciples and Jesus shared the silence; a time of contemplation, it seems to me, an inexpressible time, a blessed time. Doubtless this was the very rest proposed by Jesus to the disciples, a rest perhaps similar to the rest experienced by Jesus and the Gadarene before the villagers arrived, the Gadarene silent, seated, clothed and in his right mind, alone with Jesus.

"He was moved to the core"

When Jesus disembarked from the boat, he found himself faced with a great crowd and was "moved to the core," as Mark tells us, using the verb *splangchnizô* which is derived from *splangchna* meaning the entrails, the seat of the emotions and affections. What exactly were Jesus' feelings at this juncture? We should perhaps hesitate:

translators tend not to speak of Jesus' "entrails" here and prefer to talk about compassion, or pity. In order to avoid the choice, some translations say simply that Jesus was "moved." Just one translation stays close to the text and says, "touched in his entrails."[14]

The translators' hesitation is understandable and stems from the way the word "entrails" can be tied variously to compassion, pity or mercy: in other New Testament texts the authors add to "entrails" a further term to specify the intent. Thus Luke talks about "entrails of mercy" (1:78, adding éléous); Paul talks about "entrails of compassion" (Col 3:12, oïktirmos). It's the context that points to one meaning or the other. Given Mark's account, I prefer to think here of compassion since Jesus found himself before a crowd left to itself without a shepherd.

One feature of our word *splangchnizô* is that, when Mark uses it, Jesus is uniquely its subject (1:41; 6:34; 8:2; 9:22). Of course everyone can be moved to the core like this, seized with compassion, but I believe that when Mark reserved the word for Jesus, it's to tell us that Jesus' compassion cannot be measured against any other human compassion.

Matthew does the same, following Mark, putting the word in no one's mouth other than Jesus (9:36; 14:14; 15:32; 20:34); however, he adds to these texts a parable in which Jesus reveals that God himself also feels compassion (18:27). For Matthew too, Jesus' compassion surpasses all human compassion because only the compassion of God can stand alongside it. Discreetly, Matthew thus reveals

14. DB lists a number of French translations; the exception is the recent translation by Chouraqui. Much the same applies to English translations, in which the standard translation is "moved with compassion." When Paul and John use the same Greek terms, the KJV translates as "bowels," eg "bowels of compassion" (1 Jn 3:17). "Moved to the core" has generally been used here.

the divine compassion of Jesus, and this was surely Mark's thought too.

This is the compassion of Jesus, beyond any human compassion.

Splangchnizô is not found in the Septuagint, and here is why. *Splangchna* (entrails) corresponds to the Hebrew word *rêhèm*, which also refers to the entrails, and more precisely to the "matrix," the seat of the great emotions: tenderness, compassion and mercy. The Hebrew verb *râham* (to be touched in the entrails) most commonly has God as its subject (32 of 40 times). Nothing can match the compassion of God, and this unites Matthew and Mark as they point to the divinity of Jesus, presenting Jesus as also of unequalled compassion. When the Septuagint avoids using *splangchnizô* to translate *râham*, it seems to me this is because it regarded the verb with its graphic meaning as too direct to speak about the emotions of God. It preferred not to choose words connected to human anatomy and therefore chose the verbs for "be compassionate" (*oïkteïrô*, cf. Exod 33:19) or "be merciful" (éléêô, cf. Deut 30:3).

Mark was a Christian of Jewish origin; he wasn't shocked by the evocation of entrails because he didn't see it in terms of anatomy but as a reference to the seat of tenderness, compassion and mercy. No doubt, his Roman readers would have been prepared by Peter and Paul to receive a word like this without being shocked.

How did Mark know that Jesus had been "moved to the core"? Simply because one day he said this very thing to his disciples, straightforwardly telling them in the presence of a crowd, "I am moved to the core" (8:2). Peter remembered this and passed it on to Mark.

What so moved Jesus here? It was the crowd so similar to sheep without a shepherd. If the crowd was like a flock of sheep, then Jesus was going to take the part of their shepherd. A shepherd gathers, calms and takes care of his flock, and this is what Jesus does by teaching the crowd. He gathers, quiets and feeds with his teaching. The picture of the shepherd is very present in the Old Testament, but is applied above all to God (Ps 23; Isa 40:11), not to the leaders of the people, who are more likely to appear as bad shepherds (Jer 10:21; Ezek 34:2ff); this again enables Mark to point discreetly to Jesus as God.

Mark's discretion is really remarkable. It was enough to use the word "shepherd" and so leave it understood that Jesus is the good shepherd, unlike the leaders of the people but like God, the true shepherd. Apart from God, is there any other shepherd who will sit down to teach the crowd at length and then feed them miraculously? With just one word Mark discreetly evokes the divinity of Jesus.

This is the Christ Mark presents us, a compassionate Christ, moved to the core. This is one of the most beautiful images of Christ, given us not only by Mark but also by Matthew and Luke, a Christ who is moved by a crowd and openly tells his disciples of his feelings, and yet also a Christ moved by a single person such as the widow of Nain grieving her only son (Luke 7:13). Is there any deeper grief than a widow's for her only son? This widow was wrapped up in her grief to the point of being unable to speak, but Jesus saw her tears, tears that speak louder than words. He was moved to the core and said simply, "Don't weep!" Then he touched the bier with his compassionate hand and called the son to rise up. All Jesus' compassion is there in his gesture and in his tone of voice.

John's account doesn't use *splangchnizô* here because, no doubt, of his sense of delicacy, but he does record the scene on Easter morning when Jesus saw the tears of a grieving Mary. John doesn't make a point of this, but Jesus' emotion is surely there in the word he spoke to the grieving woman, "Mary!" (Jn 20:16) Mary recognized him by the tenderness of his voice.

This is the Jesus who reveals the compassion of his Father in parables such as the parable of the king overcome by a deeply indebted servant (Matt 18:27) or the parable of the father overwhelmed at the return of his prodigal son (Lk 15:20). This is the Christ we discover in his compassion for the crowd here, and who in compassion teaches.

"He began to teach"

Mark doesn't tell us the content of this teaching since the important thing is to know that it was teaching given compassionately, teaching that took account of the crowd's suffering and brought comfort. Teaching like this cannot be described. We need to learn to receive Jesus' teaching as teaching that is full of the compassion of someone who understands our suffering and who consoles us. He is the divine shepherd who cares for his flock, just as God the good shepherd cares for his people. It was important for Mark to bring out the compassionate nature of the teaching as he addressed his gospel to the community in Rome that was grieving its shepherds, Peter and Paul, but was cared for by Jesus, the divine shepherd.

The passage in which Jesus says, "I am moved to my core" (8:2), is the account of the second multiplication of loaves. On that occasion, his compassion impelled him not to teach but only to feed the crowd in the same way as on this first occasion. The two accounts work together: Jesus in his compassion teaches or feeds, but either way he does it because he is the shepherd who cares for his people, either by nourishing them with the word or with bread. The bread Jesus gives here is filled with his compassion.

The first account of the multiplication of loaves

This passage is too rich, so I will have to leave some of it aside in order to focus resolutely on the divine figure of Jesus. As all the commentators point out, the passage is both rooted in the past and opens onto the future, which makes it a little more difficult. In many of its details, this miracle refers back to the miracle of the manna given to Israel when in the wilderness (Exod 16:1ff); it also refers to the miracle of the multiplication of loaves at the time of Elisha (2 Kgs 4:42). However, the miracle also points forward to the Holy Supper, in particular because of the four parallel actions Jesus performs: he takes bread and after blessing it, he breaks it and gives it to the disciples. Rather than go into a verse by verse look at the multiplication itself, and because the passage is well known to all, I prefer to make a few remarks, firstly about the connections with the past and then those to do with the future; we won't forget the actual circumstances of the text, and will always have in mind the divine figure of Jesus.

A factor which shows that this passage is not solely looking either back or forward, and that it concerns a present reality is the mention of the fish. There were five loaves, but there were also two fish. The fish are part of the miracle and were multiplied just as were the loaves. However, in the Exodus, in the case of Elisha, and also at the Last Supper, there were no fish. They point neither back nor forward, but belong to the present of the event reported by Mark. However, the role of the fish is secondary compared with the loaves. The emphasis on the loaves is because they connect to both past and future; indeed it is because the loaves are involved that there is this connection.

We will begin by looking at the past.

The miracle of the Exodus (Exod 16)

After the departure from Egypt, Israel found themselves in the "desert" (Exod 16:1), just as the crowd here is in a "deserted place." The phrase is not exactly the same, but the idea is. The people in the desert were hungry and began to complain (16:2). God heard their murmuring and informed Moses that he would "rain down bread from heaven" (16:4), manna (16:31). The events are very similar because here too there was a whole crowd, a "great crowd" as Mark puts it. The description "great" seems to have been used to give the crowd a size similar to what there must have been in the desert. As in the desert, the crowd was hungry and too far from the towns to be able to obtain food.

All this is similar, but here the people don't ask for anything; there is no murmuring, and in fact no action. It's the disciples who show concern. The greatest difference is in the roles of Moses and Jesus, and it is this that most interests me. It was not Moses who brought about the miracle of the manna but God and him alone; Moses says this very thing to the people: "This is the bread the Lord has given you for food" (16:15) If we are to make a comparison with the Exodus, it is to show us that Jesus fills the same role as God, not Moses; it is Jesus who performs the miracle.

Once again, Mark does not underscore Jesus' divinity, he merely suggests it. He is discreet, leaving us to make the connection and conclude that Jesus is indeed God, the one who so extraordinarily feeds his people.

The miracle of the loaves in the time of Elisha (2 Kgs 4:42ff)

When Elisha performed the miracle of the loaves, he took matters into his own hands, as Jesus did here. Elisha told his servant to give food out to eat (4:42), as Jesus did with the disciples. But this is not the whole story. The situation is similar, but the continuation is unequivocal: when Elisha performed the miracle he puts God right there in the middle with a clearly prophetic formula: "Thus says the Lord: they will eat and there will be food left over." Therefore the miracle was performed by Elisha in the name of the Lord God. Here, there is nothing like that: Jesus does not carry himself like a prophet but as one with more authority than the prophets. He didn't act in the name of God but on his own authority. If he is above the prophets, who can he be but God himself? The miracles accomplished by the prophets were always in the name of God, but Jesus' miracles, never. Whether we compare Jesus with Moses or with Elisha, these Old Testament comparisons leave us with his divinity in view, a divinity which Mark happily leads us to discover as food for contemplation.

The miracle now

As we leave the past and before we look to the future aspects of the miracle, we will examine events at the level of their present reality, what happened.

Amazingly, there was no reaction from the crowd to the miracle performed by Jesus. There was no wonderment as there had been following the miracle of the paralytic (2:12) or in the great number of Jesus' miracles (5:42; 6:51; 7:37. . .). Mark doesn't report praise or any form of acclamation as a reaction. The account concludes strangely with a statement of the number of people present and the baskets of leftovers, twelve baskets full and five thousand men. This certainly enables us to see that this was much greater than the events of Elisha's time when only a hundred men were fed; the conclusion tells us the size of the miracle, but — no marveling from the crowd or even the disciples. Furthermore, we learn from the continuation that the disciples had not in fact understood the miracle, as Mark notes a few verses later: "They had not understood the miracle of the loaves" (6:52). This leaves us a little perplexed!

The miracle was so little understood by the disciples that Jesus, as a good teacher, had in a way to do it again. Mark goes on to report a second multiplication of loaves that took place before another crowd but the same disciples (8:1–9), again without apparent enthusiasm from the crowd, and finishing with another simple count: seven baskets and four thousand men. The continuation of the gospel shows that the disciples still had not understood, as Jesus pointed out to them, perhaps himself astonished at this incomprehension (8:17–20). The short dialogue that Mark reports between Jesus and the disciples closes with a question from Jesus: "Do you still not understand?" The question went unanswered; clearly the disciples had indeed not understood!

What needed to be understood? I believe that this incomprehension is pointed out to show that the two miracles of multiplication of loaves could not be understood until the moment of a final sharing of bread between Jesus and, this time, the disciples alone, which is to say at the institution of the Supper; and that it is with the Supper that all would become clear. This invites us, it seems to me, to examine the account of the multiplication of loaves with eyes now turned to the future, to the passage about the Supper in which we find the four important verbs: "Having <u>taken</u> the bread and after <u>blessing</u> it, he <u>broke</u> it and <u>gave</u> it to them" (14:22). This suite of verbs enables us to contemplate Jesus in his mystery. This is where I will now fix my attention.

The account of the institution of the Supper (14:22–25)

We will now occupy ourselves with a comparison of the four verbs as found in the two multiplications of bread and in the account of the Supper. I will basically leave aside Matthew and Luke with their parallel texts since these texts are later than Mark's gospel. However, I don't wish to ignore the text in which Paul reports the institution of the Supper in the first letter to the Corinthians since this text is actually prior to Mark's gospel, where it is specifically referenced. It is very likely that the Roman Christians knew this letter and perhaps Paul's text was even part of the Roman eucharist liturgy, which they would have known. We will now compare the three texts from Mark and the one from Paul (Mark 6:30 ff; 8:1ff; 14:22 ff; 1 Cor 11).

The miracle of the loaves

Before anything else it seems important to see just where in the account of the multiplication of loaves the miracle takes place. Which word or phrase tells us? In the case of the paralytic, the miracle is reported in the words "get up" and then "he got up." With the demoniac, we find it here: "come out of the man" and "they came out." What about the miracle of the loaves. In what terms is it reported?

We always speak of the "multiplication of loaves," but these terms come from modern editors and not from Mark himself. Where are the terms "multiplication" or "multiply"? Nowhere. Mark uses neither term nor their synonyms. The same applies to the parallel accounts in Matthew, Luke and even John: none of them talk about multiplication, no more in the account of the first multiplication than in the second! This is really amazing. Nevertheless, multiplication is what happened: we have only to look at the outcome — baskets full of leftovers, when to begin there were only a few loaves and thousands of seated people! What exactly does Mark say about this multiplication, which must surely be signaled somewhere in the account?

"After taking the five loaves and the two fish and lifting his eyes to heaven, he blessed and broke the loaves and gave them to the disciples" (6:41); that's all. Jesus did no more than give the disciples the bread he had broken. Nothing says that Jesus multiplied the loaves or the fish. What did the disciples then do with what Jesus had handed them? "They offered it round" (*paratithémi*).

The verb *paratithémi*, often translated as "distribute," more precisely means "offer" or "present," but not "multiply." The disciples offered the crowd broken, not multiplied, loaves, as with the fish. Whether the word is translated as "distribute" or "offer," one can but realize that the loaves were indeed multiplied if they fed such a great crowd, and multiplied to such an extent that there were basketfuls of leftovers. But when exactly were they multiplied?

It's evident from the passage that the miracle took place between the four actions of Jesus recorded by Mark (take, bless, break, give) and the distribution by the disciples. It took place in a gap in the text, in the inexpressible, because Mark has no words to describe or formulate what happened. When Mark says that Jesus broke the loaves, this doesn't mean that he multiplied them. The miracle belongs to a place beyond words. The verb "multiply" does exist in Hebrew (*râvav*) as in Greek (*plèthunô*), as we see in a verse from the psalms: "Our flocks multiply by their thousands, by tens of thousands" (Ps 144:13); so it seems to me that if Mark is unable to find human words to speak of such a miracle it's because it has to do not with us but with God. It was a divine work, a work which is beyond anything we are able to say. The miracle invites us to contemplate the inexpressible work of God.

But who actually performed the miracle? The account places the miracle between Jesus handing out the broken bread and the distribution by the disciples, in a moment beyond our grasp. I have a problem saying that the disciples performed the miracle. Mark invites us to believe that it was Jesus who did it. If this miracle was divine and beyond expression, and if it was indeed Jesus who performed what is a divine work, this discreetly once again reveals that Jesus is God.

It also seems right to add that the miracle accomplished by Jesus took place with such humility that it didn't become apparent in the hands of Jesus but in the hands of the disciples when they offered and distributed the bread to the crowd. I believe that it was only when they began to distribute the bread that they realized that the loaves had been multiplied or were multiplying as the distribution proceeded. Here is John Chrysostom on the miracle: "Once broken, the five loaves were placed in the hands of the disciples, and in their hands they spontaneously expanded as though from a fountain, in the most wonderful way" (*Homilies on the gospel of Saint Matthew, 49:3*). In choosing the verb *pègazô* (gush forth as from a spring) rather than *plèthunô* (to multiply), John Chrysostom rightly sensed that only a metaphor could invoke the inexpressible; further, this metaphor lets it be understood that the miracle was not from the disciples but from Jesus, the true life-spring (*pègè*).

Jesus is so humble that he steps back to let the miracle appear in the disciples' hands, not his. In a way, Jesus associated the disciples with the miracle in order to efface himself behind them. What humility!

This humility of Christ is found in other miracles, as in the healing of the man born blind (Jn 9:6–7): when Jesus smeared the blind man's eyes with mud and sent him to wash, the miracle was not yet apparent. The blind man became aware of it after he had washed his eyes. He came back to Jesus, who had disappeared; he "self-eclipsed"[15] in the most complete humility.

When Jesus sent the Syro-Phoenician woman home, no one could possibly have known about her daughter's healing. Only when she got home, far from Jesus, did she discover the miracle (7:30). Here again, Jesus' humility is revealed. It's an overwhelming humility that surpasses any other!

In the other account of multiplication of loaves, exactly the same takes place: "After Jesus had taken the seven loaves, and after giving thanks, he broke them and gave them to his disciples to present them to the crowd" (8:6). Once more, Jesus effaces himself and entrusts the miracle to the disciples; again, the miracle no doubt became apparent not before, but during the distribution.

In Luke's gospel, there is just the one multiplication of loaves (9:16), but it unfolds exactly as in Mark. As for Matthew, he makes things even more inexpressible because in each of the multiplications he suppresses the word "offer": "He broke the loaves and gave them to the disciples, and the disciples to the crowd" (14:19 and 15:36).

This self-effacement of Jesus is truly wonderful. That Jesus should do this is nothing new to us; in the account of the paralytic, we have also seen Jesus step back behind his Father to enable us to contemplate the Father in synergy

15. Translating the French literally.

with him. New here is that Jesus doesn't include the Father but does include the disciples, as though he was inviting them to participate in the miracle in synergy with him, honoring them to the highest degree, especially when we find in the continuation that the disciples had not understood the miracle at all! Even when drawn into the second multiplication of loaves, the disciples still failed to understand what Jesus had done in conjunction with them or through them. The humble Jesus effaces himself behind disciples who don't understand. It's shocking. The truth is that we do no better today: how often is the Lord at work through us, even at times working miracles through us, and we don't understand what he is doing! Lord Jesus, have pity on us!

It's important that we know all this when we look at the way the miracle of the loaves prepared the disciples for the miracle of the Supper, and as we prepare ourselves for the celebration of this holy Supper. What is going on at the Supper? The bread is broken, but who by? Well, it's broken by the officiant, but more exactly by Christ through the officiant, in a way that escapes our understanding. What does Paul actually say about the Supper? "The bread which we break" (1 Cor 10:16). Why "we"? To signify that the officiant and Jesus break the bread together. Then the bread is distributed but not multiplied as here in the deserted place. At the Supper, the miracle takes place elsewhere, in a manner still more inexpressible. At the Supper, Jesus breaks the bread through the officiant, but doesn't multiply it; what he does is give himself in the broken and distributed bread!

Reader friend, we are to remain humbly uncomprehending of what is beyond us and content ourselves with contemplating Christ in the infinite mystery of his humble presence, his so humble presence! Not only does Christ efface himself behind the disciples to work through them, but he also effaces himself to give himself in the bread that is distributed. If there are no words to express the miracle of multiplication, neither are there any for the Supper.

If the multiplication of the loaves was a miracle, the Supper is greater still. The miracle of the multiplication is inexpressible; with how much more reason is that true of the Supper. It is a miracle I prefer to contemplate rather than attempt to analyze. I leave analysis to the theologians and prefer to remain in silence before the mystery, the Supper as much as the multiplication.

If there are no words to express the miracle of multiplication, it seems to me this is because it contains the miracle of the Supper; these two inexpressible miracles mutually illuminate and involve each other. There is a miracle here beyond any other miracle. What an unfathomable mystery envelops the very being of Jesus who gives himself in the broken bread!

The interrelation between the multiplication and the Supper is finely stated by Macarius the great (4th century), not in one word but in a phrase that brings them together: "He changed the nature of the five loaves from five into a multitude" (Homily 44/2). How wonderful this is: the reference to multiplication is in the words "five loaves into a multitude," and the reference to the Supper in the words "he changed the nature of the loaves." Macarius underlines the interrelation between the two inseparable miracles even as he leaves them both in the inexpressible. This is truly of great spiritual depth!

The actions in the multiplication and the Supper

In order to better contemplate the mystery of the multiplication, we will pause a little over Jesus' actions and their connection with the Supper: taking bread, blessing , breaking and giving it out. There are some differences between the words used here and at the Supper. We will compare four texts: the two accounts of multiplication, the account of the Last Supper and the Eucharistic liturgy reported by Paul. In order not to be over-burdened, we will leave aside the gospels of Matthew, Luke and John, each of which is more recent than Mark.

Mark 6:41 : take, lift the eyes, bless, break, give

Mark 8:6 : take, give thanks, break, give

Mark 14:22 : take, bless, break, give

1 Cor 11:24 : take, give thanks, break

Two of the verbs are present in the three gospel texts, reinforcing the connection between them, "take" and "give."

"Bless" and "give thanks" alternate, acting so to speak as synonyms.

"Break" is there in all four.

I assume that the foundational text is Paul's in his letter written a dozen years before Mark's gospel; Mark leans on the letter, faithful to his spiritual master.

At the same time, we should also consider foundational what Mark received orally from his other master, Peter, who was present at each of the multiplications as well as the Supper. For his part, Paul was not there, but what he wrote about the Supper, he says he received from the Lord, which is to say, Jesus: "What I received from the Lord," he says as he introduces his text on the Supper (11:23). How did he receive it? By revelation or from the mouth of a witness? I don't know, but we can have confidence in him. Certainly, this text is particularly important since it was received from Jesus.

"He took" and "he gave"

"Having taken the loaves": this is a constant in these accounts. "He gave" is not in Paul's text, but we can think of it as understood because in the celebration of the Supper, the bread is always "given." The action happened even if it is not expressly stated.

"Having taken the loaves": it was not for himself that Jesus took the bread, not to consume it himself, but to give to the disciples for them to give to the crowd. Jesus took in order to give; this is why I choose to study the two verbs together. At the Supper, the same happens: Jesus takes the bread, again to give; again he gives to the disciples. He keeps nothing for himself. Mark tells us this with great simplicity, as if to show us the great simplicity with which Jesus acted: take, bless, break, give . . . They are indeed actions of great simplicity!

"He gave": at the time of the multiplication of the loaves, Jesus did this silently. At the Supper, he performed the same actions but accompanying them with a very simple word, "Take." Everything lies in the simplicity of the words, but what depth in this simplicity when we listen to what follows: "Take, this is my body!" As he gave the bread, he gave his life; he gave himself. The mystery of his life is there, in the piece of bread that is given me. The words are both simple and unfathomable.

At the multiplication of the loaves, Jesus performed the simple act of giving and did so in silence; this silence is already full of an infinite mystery. When Mark tells us later that the disciples had not understood the multiplication at all (6:52), what could they have understood? Jesus' actions were freighted with meaning at that point beyond under-standing because it was before the Supper; it was only with the Supper that all became clear to them. But then also . . . what about us after the Holy Supper? Do we really under-stand the depth of Jesus' actions?

"He gave the bread to the disciples": in giving the bread, Jesus gives himself . . . What infinite mystery! It is an unfathomable mystery if we consider that it was his divine-human life that he gives in giving the bread! And what love in this simple act! "There is no greater love than to give your life for your friends" (Jn 15:13).

"Having lifted his eyes to heaven"

"He blessed" or "he gave thanks": the texts alternate here. On one hand, Paul says that Jesus gave thanks, which Mark also says in the second multiplication of loaves. On the other hand, Mark employs a second verb, very close it's true, which he perhaps had from Peter: "bless." Mark uses it for the first multiplication and for the Supper. But before examining these two verbs, both verbs of prayer, we should consider a verb introduced by Mark only here in the first passage: "Having lifted his eyes to heaven." What are we to say about this addition, which again Mark must have received from Peter?

Firstly, it is almost superfluous: the prayer of blessing or giving thanks is the same whether Jesus' eyes were lifted to heaven or not. Perhaps this is why Mark doesn't re-use this expression in 8:6 or 14:22? Nevertheless, that he uses it here is doubtless because he stood by what he received from Peter and wanted the phrase to have its place. And indeed, what Peter understood when he saw Jesus lift his eyes to heaven is very important.

"Having lifted his eyes to heaven": Jesus turned his face to heaven, which is to say to God. We know that it was a Jewish custom to say "heaven" rather than "God" since it avoided naming God. It was out of respect for God that his most holy name was not to be pronounced by impure lips. Mark, of Jewish origin, retained this highly respectful way of speaking of God, as we see for example in 8:11, "a sign came from heaven," which is to say from God; or 11:30: "Does the baptism come from heaven (that is from God) or from men?" It's the same here: to lift one's eyes to heaven is to lift them to God. In saying this, Mark discreetly draws our attention to the presence of God, which is wonderful because God is not named in this passage. We could believe him to be absent. Jesus heavenward look invites us to consider God as present. God is unseen and says nothing; that doesn't mean he isn't there in the inexpressible.

Wonderful! Lifting his eyes to God, his Father, Jesus in this sense calls on his Father to be associated with what was going on. He already had the loaves in his hands, and it was with the bread in his hands that he turned to his Father. There is a very strong bond of love between the Son and the Father. Peter had seen this love on Jesus' face as he turned to heaven and had made careful note; he invites us to contemplate the Son lifting his eyes full of love to the Father.

For Jesus, at this moment, his Father was there, but above him, in heaven. Events were to take place in the humility of the Son who is located far below, on the earth. The humble Jesus!

Nothing says that the Father turned his face to his Son since this really touches on the inexpressible, but I believe that we can suppose it to be the case and so contemplate the Father and the Son looking at each other in this powerful moment that announces the Supper.

"You are my beloved Son," the Father said on the day of the baptism, from heaven (1:11). Jesus was silent as he listened to these words. Here, he lifts his eyes to the one who had spoken with such love, and we can but sense an infinite love in Jesus' face turned to his Father. Peter had noticed this and it was engraved on his heart, with reason, because it was most unusual to see Jesus so lift his eyes to his Father; Peter had seen it, and could not forget .What was engraved on his heart, he transmitted to Mark,who in turn reported it to us. We need to remember this in the celebration of the Supper; it is the moment the Father and the Son are united. We can guard in our hearts this profound mystery which will one day be revealed: the Father and the Son closely united.

"Having lifted his eyes to heaven": this was the attitude in which Jesus prayed. But which was it, blessing or giving thanks?

"He blessed" or "he gave thanks"

Mark doesn't report Jesus' words, not giving us the contents of his prayer, not in the account of the first or second multiplication, not in the account of the Supper, and neither does Paul say anything in the letter to the Corinthians. We therefore don't know if Jesus spoke a Jewish liturgical prayer or if it was improvised. It would be interesting to know, but it remains in the secret intimacy between the Father and the Son since it was to his Father that Jesus addressed the prayer, his face turned towards him. Even if he was praying in front of the whole crowd and it was liturgical prayer known to everyone, the prayer retains an intimate aspect, just as much in the intimacy of the Father and the Son as his prayers in solitude in another deserted place (1:35) or on a mountain (6:46). We humbly accept not knowing and have no business meddling with the intimacy at the heart of the Trinity.

Here, with the first multiplication, Mark uses the verb "bless," as he does for the Supper. The verb bless is interesting here because it is very commonly followed by a complement. Here though there is none stated, so we have to see if perhaps there is a complement left understood. This can indeed be the case, and if it's so here, we might hesitate between "he blessed God" and "he blessed the loaves." The two are possible (see Luke 1:64 for "bless God" and Luke 9:16 for "bless the loaves"). Jesus had just lifted his eyes to his Father and so might be blessing him; he was also holding the loaves in his hands and so might also have been blessing them. According to Luke, it was the loaves that Jesus blessed (9:16). Some translations add the word "God" here, so for them this word was understood. I tend to think that if the complement here is understood, it might be because it has to do with the inexpressible. If so, this "inexpressible" is God and not the bread. Out of respect for God, Mark tells us that Jesus turned his eyes "to heaven"; and again out of the same respect he keeps back his name, leaving us in contemplation of the Son blessing the Father.

Perhaps, though, the understood complement is there to invite us to have both in mind, that Jesus blessed both his Father and the bread, which doesn't comport badly with what we have just been saying. Jesus blesses the Father for the bread he received from the disciples, from the Father through them. He also blesses the bread which would have such a profound meaning after the Supper when he would say, "This is my body." Jesus already had the perspective of the Supper in his heart when he lifted his eyes to heaven in the midst of the crowd in this deserted place, the bread in his hands. But we mustn't go too far;

Mark's unstated complement calls us to contemplation and adoration: there Jesus is, the loaves in his hands and his eyes turned to his Father.

"He gave thanks": the same applies as to the verb "bless." When Mark (8:6) and Paul (1 Cor 11:24) say that Jesus gave thanks with no complement, it could mean that "he gave thanks to God" and equally "he gave thanks for the bread." We could make the same comments as with "bless."

"He broke the loaves"

"He broke": this verb merits our full attention; we will examine it closely.

In all the biblical texts where we find bread being broken (15 in all, including 8:6; 14:22 and 1 Cor 11:24), the verb *klaô* is used. The sole exception is here, with the first multiplication of loaves (as in the parallel passage in Luke 9:16) where we find the composite verb *kataklaô*, which is derived from *klaô*.

To this point, in the translations I have been able to consult, I have not found any difference of meaning being made between the two verbs.[16] Everyone translates the two Greek terms by just one word, "break." I too cannot see how to do any better in the sense that language is limited here. Even Jerome translated the two Greek verbs by the same Latin verb *frango*. However, there must be a difference in Greek between the simple verb and the composite. It must be so because I don't otherwise see why Mark would have this one usage here and not use a phrase which was rooted in custom; so, that there is a difference is factual, as indeed is stated by Bailly in his dictionary. In fact there

16. When DB discusses French translations, the same is true of English translations.

is a very surprising difference, one which immerses me in wonderment and adoration. What exactly is it?

We note first that Paul uses the simple verb *klaô* for the phrase "break bread" as found in the Septuagint (Jer 16:7). We can understand that Paul wouldn't want to abandon the classic expression since he hadn't seen Jesus break the bread at this first multiplication. When Mark wrote his first multiplication account he didn't depend on either Paul or the Septuagint; he was passing on what Peter, who had been present had told him. No doubt Peter had noted something particular in the way Jesus broke the loaves. How then had he broken them? It can't have been as per normal according to the Jewish way since the customary method is always expressed by *klaô*. Peter must have remembered clearly that at this first multiplication and not at the second, Jesus had broken the bread in an unusual way. What did he do? How had he broken the loaves?

The verb *kataklaô* certainly means "to break" but it has an extra meaning, "to break with emotion." Bailly specifies that there is indeed a certain emotion in the manner of breaking, an emotion that will vary according to the context: pain, sorrow, fear, passion etc. The only use of the verb in the Septuagint is in a complaint of God concerning his people who are compared to a vine. God laments to see his vine "broken," which is to say "smashed" (*katakalaô*) with anger by the enemy. The mention of anger specifies the emotion involved (Ezek 19:12).

With this verb *katakalaô*, we discover that Jesus broke the bread with emotion, an emotion sufficiently open for Peter to have noted it. What emotion? We must bear in mind that Jesus had the bread in his hands and perhaps his eyes turned to his Father. This bread was not just any bread; for Jesus it was bread that announced the Holy Supper about which he would say "this is my body." I don't know with what emotion Jesus broke the bread but it is clear that he must have broken it with real emotion, an emotion that certainly escapes me but which Peter noticed and didn't know how to define other than by using *katakalaô* when he talked to Mark. Certainly God the Father perceived and understood. It's enough for me to know that the emotion passed between the Father and the Son in the inexpressible of their relationship.

In the second account of multiplication, Peter hadn't seen the same emotion in Jesus, although Jesus himself states the strong emotion he then experienced: "I am moved to the core for this crowd" (8:2). Was this the same emotion as on the first occasion? I don't know, but for sure Jesus experienced both occasions with his whole heart.

When Jesus broke the bread, the prayer addressed to the Father had finished; he broke the bread in silence, in a silence full of an emotion that escapes us. The prefix *kata* added to the verb *klaô* denotes a movement downwards, to the deeps. I believe this is a way of telling us that this emotion of Jesus was profound, that it came from the depths of his being. This is the way in which Jesus broke the bread. I can say nothing more.

When he wrote his account of the first multiplication of loaves, Matthew was inspired by Mark, but while he must have noted this verb *katakalaô* he choose not to retain it. Matthew, though present that day, had not noticed what Peter saw in Jesus' actions. I believe there is no other explanation to give than this: Jesus emotion at the moment of breaking the bread was sufficiently perceptible for Peter to take note, but sufficiently restrained for it to escape Matthew's attention.

Multiplication of the loaves and the holy Supper

Reader friend, I have given it to be understood numerous times that Jesus was already thinking of the Holy Supper at the moment the bread was multiplied. I have said this as though it was quite obvious, but it is not really so evident. How can we know if Jesus was already thinking of the Supper in this deserted place? Mark doesn't say anything that specifically points us in this direction. However certain Church Fathers thought that the Supper was already in Jesus' heart. Ephraim the Syrian, among others, thought so and tells us that Jesus multiplied the loaves to prepare the disciples for the Supper: "In the desert, Our Lord multiplied the bread, and at Cana he turned the water into wine. He thus accustomed the disciples' mouths to his bread and his wine until the time came for him to give them his body and his blood." (*Commentary on the Diatessaron,* XII, 1, SC 121, p 213).

Ephraim doesn't state his source for saying this. No, he was a blessed man whose spiritual intuition was enough. There was no point him arguing the point as we are obliged to do today. For the Fathers, spiritual intuition sufficed, so exegetical argument is not what we look for in the Fathers but rather the spiritual authority they received from the Holy Spirit, and this leads to the inspired nature of their commentaries. In truth, their lives are sufficient testimony. This is the case with Ephraim: the spiritual authority he received from the Holy Spirit is enough for us to accept what he says.

I don't have this authority, and following our modern method of doing exegesis, I have to proceed by argumentation. I will continue to submit to this discipline the best I can.

In fact, Ephraim had no need to argue this point, no more really than do we; he only needed to stick with what we read in John's gospel. This gospel reports the multiplication of loaves (6:1–15) along with a lengthy discourse by Jesus the next day (6:23–58); this discourse is a sort of commentary on the multiplication, telling us that Jesus really was thinking of the Holy Supper at the time of the multiplication. It was in this discourse that Jesus said, "I am the bread of life . . . Whoever eats my body and drinks my blood has eternal life" (6:35, 54). For Ephraim, John's gospel was his reference; this is clear and I understand. He was right. But, you may say to me, John's gospel is much later than Mark's . . . Indeed! So we will continue with Mark's gospel.

As we do so, we start with a point that Mark himself makes, that the disciples hadn't understood the miracle of the loaves (6:52). Particularly beyond their understanding was Jesus' silence as he broke the bread. Jesus broke the loaves without saying anything. The silence is so surprising because in the Jewish liturgy the breaking of bread at the beginning of a meal was always accompanied by a liturgical word. The first three gospels and Paul are together in making it clearly understood that Jesus broke the loaves in silence. He broke them after giving thanks and not while doing so. If it had been at the same time, the verb "bless" (or "give thanks" depending on the gospel) would be a participle and the verb "break" indicative. In the three gospels, though, both verbs are indicative with a conjunction (*kaï*) between them, and this expresses succession. For his part, Paul does use the participle for "giving thanks," but it is an aorist participle, which puts it in the past. The translations are correct to say that Jesus broke the loaves after giving thanks. In short, Jesus would have been expected to speak as he broke the bread but did not. Why this silence?

The use of *kataklaô* seems decisive to me since it breaks with custom. The verb reveals genuine emotion which is not foreseen by the liturgy, a sudden emotion at the moment of breaking the bread. It is this that impels Jesus to be silent; he wished to contain his feelings.

This silence and emotion as the bread is broken remained incomprehensible to the disciples until the evening before his death; then, during the Supper, he took the bread again and broke it. At this moment he was no longer silent and now said, "This is my body." Everything now became clear to the disciples; it is just this statement that must have risen up in Jesus' heart and filled him with emotion the day the loaves were multiplied. He was already thinking of the Supper without being able to mention it to the disciples because the hour had not yet come. We get a glimpse of this in Mark, and John's gospel wonderfully clarifies and confirms: Jesus was thinking of the Supper in the event of the multiplied bread.

Jesus' actions as he broke the bread while responding emotionally to the thought of the Supper particularly holds my attention: the whole of the Passion was in view. At the multiplication Jesus was silent as he broke the loaves. The disciples and the crowd were also silent, still without understanding. But Mark and his readers understand well enough the depth of this action and it brings them to silence too: at every Holy Supper, the bread is broken anew. This gospel was written for us, and it was also for us that Jesus broke the bread; and it is for us too to contemplate in silence this act of unfathomable depth. It is his life that he gives us in giving us the bread. "There is no greater love than to give your life for your friends" (John 15:13).

The miracle of the loaves, his inexpressible miracle, beyond any other, is much greater and deeper than simply a multiplication of bread; it contains in it the Supper.

After the multiplication of loaves, and to help the disciples understand the miracle, Jesus drew their attention to a point that merits ours too: "'When I broke the five loaves for the five thousand, don't you remember how many baskets full of scraps you collected?' They replied, 'Twelve'" (8:18–19). At the time the disciples failed to understand why Jesus had asked this question. After the Last Supper, though, no doubt they understand that the twelve baskets of leftovers were for them, the twelve disciples, with enough left to distribute the Supper throughout the earth and for all time.

Lord Jesus,
you led your disciples into the silence of the desert
to let them enjoy a time of retreat with you,
and you chose this moment to lead them along paths
they never expected.
You wrote on their hearts in silence unforgettable acts
the Holy Spirit little by little led them to understand.

Before breaking the bread in this deserted place
you turned your face in silence to the Father
in loving communion with him, he silent too,
the Holy Spirit uniting you in the depths of the silence.

After giving thanks, you broke the bread in silence,
in loving communion with the crowd
who came to be fed of this bread in silence,
the Holy Spirit uniting you in the depths of the silence.

After breaking the bread you gave it in silence to the disciples,
who received it and passed it in silence on to the crowd
the Holy Spirit uniting you all in the depths of this silence.

And in your heart already in profile stood the cross waiting
*   in silence.*

Lord Jesus, each holy Supper I am silent
and contemplate you breaking the bread,
in loving communion with your Father,
with the disciples, the crowd
and with we who receive the broken bread.
May the Holy Spirit pursue his work in our hearts
uniting us with you in the deeps of this communion of love.

And may that day at last come when you break the
    bread anew
with us and for us in the Kingdom of your Father;
may this blessed day come
when we contemplate you, receiving from you the bread,
I pray this of you who live and reign with the Father and
    Holy Spirit
now and always throughout the ages. Amen.

THE PASSION ANNOUNCED

(MARK 8:27-33)

27. Jesus went with his disciples into the villages of Caesarea Philippi. Along the way, he questioned the disciples, saying to them, "Who do people say I am?" 28. They replied, "John the Baptist, others Elijah or another of the prophets." 29. He asked them, "And you, who do you say I am?" Peter, answering, said, "You are the Christ." 30. He commanded them severely not to say this to anyone. 31. Then he began to teach them that it was necessary that the Son of Man suffer many things, be rejected by the elders, the chief priests and scribes, that he be killed, but that three days later he would rise. 32. He said this openly. Peter took him aside and began to rebuke him. 33. He turned around and, looking at the disciples, he rebuked Peter and said, "Get behind me Satan; you don't consider the things of God but the things of men."

THIS VERY WELL-KNOWN DIALOGUE BETWEEN JESUS AND the disciples is without doubt the most important of all the dialogues in Mark's gospel; the most important because it contains the announcement of the death and resurrection of Christ. That the Christ should die was for some a real blasphemy, for others a scandal, but for us wonderful good news because this death is victorious over death. I'm going to look closely only at verse 31, but without ignoring the rest of the passage, in particular Peter's second little speech and Jesus' response.

This one verse, verse 31, reports the Passion of Jesus, his death and his resurrection, which is to say, the very heart of his life. Not only is this the heart of Jesus' life, but also the heart of the New Testament and, I believe, the heart of the whole Bible.

It is surprising to see how such an important subject is treated here by Jesus so briefly: just one verse, one short statement addressed solely to the disciples. It is extremely brief, but also dense and profound. This invites us to pause over each word, seeking to go beyond the surface meaning and look into its depths. The depths are unfathomable because the life of Jesus in his divine mystery is unfathomable . . .

This is the first time Jesus spoke of his death and his resurrection. It is he who is speaking, not the evangelist; these two things are very different. Mark reports here Jesus' own words. When I think of this, I become aware of the inestimable value of this brief statement! Who am I to approach such words? Who am I to talk about them? I therefore petition the Lord to give me the words: Lord Jesus, your life, your death, your resurrection, everything in you is such a great mystery that it is not possible for me to speak of them without the help of the Holy Spirit. May he come now and, in his grace, illumine for me things infinitely beyond me, help me to speak of them correctly; I pray this of you who live and reign with the Father and with the Holy Spirit, now and ever, throughout all ages. Amen.

The final part of the dialogue shows us that Jesus' announcement was badly received because it was shocking. For Peter, and no doubt equally so for the other disciples, and even for us, the announcement of the Passion was and is hard to receive.

Why was Jesus so brief about such an important matter? Because it was a very difficult subject to engage, for two reasons.

Firstly, because it was difficult for the disciples to understand, and Peter's reaction demonstrates this. That Jesus be put to death, murdered, was unacceptable, contrary to everything the disciples could have expected. It was inadmissible and indeed incomprehensible!

Then, secondly, because it was a difficult subject for Jesus to broach. Jesus was speaking here not of some random death but of his own! To this point it was not something he had discussed. You don't talk about your own death in the way you discuss the weather! An indication of how difficult it was for Jesus is the way he hides himself, speaking not so much of himself as of a third party, the Son of Man. This effacement of self is obvious. Early in the conversation, Jesus speaks of himself in the first person, "Who *am I?*" (8:27), and then, "Who do you say *I am?*" (8:29). In these two questions, Jesus talks about himself, and then suddenly he removes himself and talks about the Son of Man! He was veiling himself like this because it was too difficult to speak of his own death; it was too hard. Not that anyone was deceived; for the disciples, like us, it is clear that he was this Son of Man.

We will now engage with this dense, profound verse.

"He began to teach them"

"He began to teach them": these words merit our full attention. The phrase is found here for the fourth time in this gospel (4:1; 6:2, 34). It's a little curious that Mark would be telling us Jesus "began" when he had already taught at length and had "begun" three times.

In order to lessen this difficulty, some translators today prefer to say "he set about teaching," which seems to fit better. While this isn't wrong, I believe it's better to keep the meaning of "begin" and its fellow, "beginning." Jesus is preparing here to say something so important that we can regard it as the beginning of the most important chapter in Christian theology. Mark introduced his gospel with the word "beginning," and this links up with the very first word of the Bible; the cross, announced here by Jesus, is the beginning of a new era. While true, this doesn't rid us of the difficulty that this is the fourth time Jesus "began" to teach.

Translating by "he began to teach" does in fact fit, even after the first three usages of the phrase. It is correct to say here that Jesus "began to teach" because the three other occasions of teaching were addressed to other audiences. This was the first time that Jesus taught the disciples. To this point, he had taught the crowds (4:1 and 6:34) or an assembly in a synagogue (6:2). Yes, the disciples had been present, but Jesus had not been addressing them directly. Here, he is only speaking to them. Mark was therefore right to say that he began to teach them; this is even more the case in that this was the first time for Jesus to broach the subject of his death and resurrection. We should accordingly keep the verb "begin" with its rich connotations: the beginning of the Bible, the beginning of Mark's gospel . . . Most translators were right to use "begin."

To say that Jesus "began to teach" also has behind it the idea that this teaching was not finished and would later be taken up again. This of course is what took place; at least twice more Jesus spoke of this subject to the same audience (9:31–32 and 10:32–34), and we, with the disciples, need to listen again; not that we need to understand what was going to happen next because Jesus had covered everything by speaking of his resurrection, but simply that we should constantly reconsider it. We will also see that Jesus returned to the subject of his death and resurrection to provide important specifics.

Why not say everything on a single occasion? Well, for the reason already mentioned: that it was too difficult for the disciples to understand and for Jesus to talk about. Jesus was aware of the difficulties; when he comes back to this teaching it is always stepping back behind the figure of the Son of Man, showing that he maintained a delicacy which taught him to speak of himself indirectly.

The difficulty in speaking about such a subject resides not in the use of complicated words because Jesus uses really simple words here, but in the way the subject touches the heart. To speak of some unknown person's death is relatively easy, but to speak of your own death to those you love, this is another matter. It's because there was love between Jesus and the disciples that Jesus had trouble speaking; what he had to say was disturbing. He preferred to go over things repeatedly rather than just once. By leaving time before picking it up again, Jesus gave the disciples time to assimilate something that was difficult for them to grasp.

Again, it's because the announcement touched on heart intimacy that Jesus chose to speak of this to the disciples alone rather than to a whole crowd. We need to bear in mind the love between Jesus and his disciples, the better to hear what Jesus is saying. I too need to be aware of this if I am to be properly accountable to you; I know that there is love between Jesus and you. May God help me and give me the necessary tact.

"To teach"

"To teach" (*didaskô*): that Jesus taught makes him a master (*didaskolos*), which is just how the disciples addressed him, calling him "master" (4:38; 9:38 . . .) many times. Not only the disciples but others spoke to him in this way, as "master" (9:17; 10:17 . . .).

As a master, though, Jesus' teaching was very different from the scribes, as the crowd were quick to note: "He teaches as one with authority and not like the scribes" (1:22). The difference is at this level of authority, as the crowd realize again, adding that he even had authority over the unclean spirits (1:27), as we have seen in the passage about the demoniac. The authority is particularly apparent because Jesus taught without depending on some other rabbi, and this was most unusual. All rabbis spoke by referring to other rabbis. The disciples had themselves seen Jesus' authority over the wind and the sea (4:41). They had seen it again when he walked on the water, which (Job 9:8) is a property of God alone; more, when walking on the water Jesus had said to them "I am," and only God had authority to say this (6:50).

The disciples knew more about Jesus than the crowd. Nonetheless, when Jesus asked, Peter said simply, "You are the Christ," unlike Thomas after the resurrection when he said, "My Lord and my God" (John 20:28). At this moment, halfway through this gospel, the divinity of Jesus was not yet completely welcomed, received, assimilated by the disciples. There is a way to understand this.

Immediately after the divine revelation of him walking on the water, Mark says that "the disciples had not yet understood the multiplication of the loaves," and then gives this explanation, "because their hearts were hardened" (6:52). Hardening of the heart, this is the major obstacle preventing an understanding or welcoming of the divinity of Christ. Here, Peter's reaction shows that he didn't understand Jesus' teaching. Jesus then reveals the source of the hardening of heart, Satan: "Get behind me, Satan." In saying this, Jesus, of course, was not speaking to Peter but to Satan, who was bullying Peter just as the unclean spirit had bullied the demoniac. Jesus didn't on this occasion say, "Come out of the man," but, "Get behind me," but this is also very strong. It was Satan who was responsible for the hardening of heart.

If we are to dislodge Satan from a place he occupies wrongly, we need to have received the Holy Spirit. For the disciples, it was only after receiving the Holy Spirit by the breath of Jesus (John 20:22) that they could fully receive the mystery of Jesus' divinity. Only after this event could Thomas say to Jesus, "My Lord and my God" (John 20:28). (BUT HE WASN'T THERE AND HADNT RECEIVED)

May the Holy Spirit help us enter into this teaching of Jesus and see it in it its divine profundity.

"The Son of Man"

We have already spoken about this, so it's not necessary to go over it again. We know that Jesus is referring to himself when he speaks of the Son of Man.

What we need to note here is that Jesus leaves out the word "Christ," which Peter had just used to say who Jesus was for him (8:29). Jesus preferred to speak not of Christ but of "the Son of Man" and would do the same in each of his announcements of the Passion. Never, in Mark's gospel, does he speak of himself by saying "the Christ"; he preferred to say "the Son of Man."

Why was Jesus distancing himself from the term Christ? It's because in Judaism, as throughout the Old Testament, the Christ was not God. However, it was not the same with the Son of Man, a figure so close to God that he could be considered a divine being, as we have previously noted. We won't return to this and will now look at what Jesus brings out in his teaching.

"It's necessary . . ."

"It is necessary": these are the first words of the teaching. It governs all that follows: "It is necessary that the Son of Man suffer greatly, that he be mistreated, that he be killed and that he rise." The Son of Man is the subject of all the following verbs but not of "it is necessary," which is impersonal.

If we translate here by "the Son of Man must suffer . . . ," we are misusing the text since it makes "the Son of Man" the subject of must, which is not correct. "It is necessary" is indeed impersonal. However, an impersonal verb hides an unnamed subject. "It is necessary" means there is a power, a will, a demand which remains hidden and is not revealed by Jesus here. Who is it that is demanding, willing, obliging, imposing on the Son of Man the need to suffer and be killed? Jesus doesn't say. Was it God, was it the Evil One or perhaps some other power?

Among the Greeks, fate (*heimarménè*) was an entity that existed; it was a real force that imposed its demands on everyone including the gods, even Zeus; it was a power no one could escape, and the Greek tragedies illustrate fate's unalterable demands. Fate was also real to the Romans, who knew it as *fatum*, so the Christians to whom Mark was writing must have been affected by this view of life. The reality of fate perhaps belongs to all the philosophies and theologies of the world apart from the biblical. No word for fate exists in Hebrew; Mark, moreover, no more than the rest of the New Testament or the whole of the Septuagint, ever uses the Greek word *heimarménè*. No one in the Bible, neither God nor people, is subject to fate.

Who then is the real subject of the "it is necessary" if not fate? Could it be God who imposes so much suffering on his Son? If it was so, this would sadism! Would it be the Son imposing it on himself? That would be masochism. Who then? Might it be the Evil One imposing on the Son of Man suffering, death and resurrection? Certainly not! Satan might impose death but not resurrection! More, the continuation of the text even shows that Satan, in Peter's mouth, opposed Jesus statement. If he rebelled against it, this shows that he was not the subject, the source; it was not he who wished Jesus to die and rise. The demands of Satan are all for death, certainly not for the resurrection of Jesus.

In fact, Satan's demands are the demands of non-love. For Jesus, any true demand came from love, and it is this demand of love, of divine love, which is the subject that means "it is necessary." Jesus was not subject to the demands of evil, only the demands of divine love. It was through love that he had to suffer and die as well as rise.

We can be more precise about the demands of love. They are not demands whose pressure comes from outside but from inside. I can say to myself, "It's necessary for me to visit this person, my heart says so." This is a demand of love, not an externally imposed demand; it springs from the depths of my heart. No one obliges me; fate has nothing to do with it. This demand, from inside, the heart demand, also exists in the heart of God. It is the requirement of his love. This demand of love is not one that the Father imposes on the Son, and neither is it self-imposed by the Son; no, it is the demand of the common love between the Father and the Son, their common demand, and indeed the common demand of the Father, the Son and the Holy Spirit, a demand of Trinitarian love. What the Father wants is what the Son wants. It is the common will of the three Persons of the Trinity, their common unanimous love. This "it is necessary" expresses the common decision of the most perfect unity of love, a decision taken by common accord in the inseparable Trinitarian unity, in the inseparable communion of love of the Father, the Son and the Holy Spirit, beyond understanding, in a union which nothing can divide. We must never forget that the Trinitarian God is one, perfectly one, inseparably one (Deut 6:4). If we lose sight of this, the announcements of the Passion are shocking and inadmissible; and God would be a perverse god.

"It is necessary that he suffer many things"

"It is necessary that he suffer many things": why is there suffering in the demands of divine love? The question seems to me to be rather, "for whom, on behalf of whom is the suffering in this love?" The Trinity would be masochistic if the suffering was for self. But that is not the case; the Trinity does not suffer for self but for us, to save us from the power of death, to save us from the grip of Satan. This, the logic of love, leads Jesus to tell us, "There is no greater love than to give your life for your friends" (John 15:13). To give one's life is the pinnacle of love, but it is a pinnacle reached through suffering, through death, through the cross. It was in order to take the demands of love to their conclusion that Jesus became a man, all the way to the cross.

Behind "it is necessary" and veiled from eyes is an infinite love which Jesus doesn't name out of delicacy and humility, but also because this love beyond any other love so surpasses words it has no name. We can pause here a while over this reality of divine love so great that it is inexpressible.

I am struck and moved that in Mark's gospel so little space is given to words about love. The noun for love (*agape*) is absent, which is really amazing. The verb form (*agapaô*) is only found six times, and five of these are in quotations from the Old Testament. This is very few compared with John's gospel where the noun is found seven times and the verb thirty five, and his first letter, with the noun eighteen times and the verb twenty seven.

Happily we have John to tell us the importance of love in Christian faith! I would add that happily there is also Mark, portraying love differently, in a complementary, not contradictory way. We need the two gospels to enrich each other.

John is the singer of love who employs every tone and every variation on love, both divine and human. As for Mark, he is the contemplative of love, who shows us that love is so great and so beautiful that there are no words to express it. For Mark, love is as inexpressible as is God since love has its source in God; love is so closely tied to God as to be inexpressible.

In Mark, Jesus is never the subject of the verb "love" except for just once, to attest that yes, Jesus loves (10:21). This needed to be said at least once, but that was enough for Mark since for him Jesus was nothing but love, full of a love beyond all other love. The one passage concerns the rich young man, and it is Mark who tells us that Jesus loved; it wasn't Jesus who said so because Jesus himself had no human words to tell the divine love that was in him. If Jesus didn't state it, how was his love perceived? It was in a look: Mark tells us, "Jesus looked at him and loved him." The love of Jesus was unspoken but filled his eyes. What a look! The verb Mark uses for "look" (*emblépô*) speaks of a way of looking (*blépô*) which penetrates deep into the heart (*en* means "into" and becomes *em* before the "b" of *blépô*), so deeply that it comes from the depths of God. It's because it's so profound that it's inexpressible. This same look of love from Jesus is next fixed on the disciples (10:27), but now Mark has no need to add that Jesus loved them because it is implicit and belongs to the indescribable. Truly, this love of Jesus is for all of us. It's up to us to understand that Mark shows us this one young man, who was hardly a model to follow, as an example. This was a man stricken with love of his money, a man who might have become a disciple but who miscarried. Well, it's this man that Jesus loved, a sign that Jesus loves everyone. Mark had no need to say more about the love of Jesus; this was enough. The rest is the unutterable love that filled the heart of Christ, as it fills the heart of God. What else does Mark say about the love of God for us? Nothing! God is never the subject of the verb, not because he doesn't love but because his love is beyond words. We are to learn to contemplate this love beyond all love. Happily again, we have John who tells us that God "so loved the world" (3:16), but this "so loved" is still nothing compared with the inexpressible; it is still just a pale reflection of a reality infinitely deeper.

This, it seems to me, is what Mark brings to our reflections on love. His apparent poverty of speech is in fact a great richness. His silence on the subject is very eloquent.

This inexpressible love is the interior power hidden in "it is necessary," the interior power which impelled and animated Jesus on his journey to the cross.

The suffering of the Passion

"It is necessary that he suffer greatly": with this expression, Jesus announces the suffering of the Passion, immense suffering which becomes apparent in Mark's account of the Passion. It is true that Jesus suffered greatly during his Passion. The very word "passion" comes from the Latin *passio* which means "suffering." Everything the gospel describes, the whipping, the slaps and the crucifixion, reveals the physical suffering. To this must be added the moral and emotional suffering, the suffering of being betrayed, denied, abandoned, mocked, ridiculed . . . Let's not insist; Jesus was indeed a man of sorrows.

It's because he loved that he followed the demands of love to their end; it's because he loved that Jesus bore and endured the suffering of the cross, out of love for us. It was in love for Peter and love for us that he bore betrayal. It's the logic of love to be exposed to suffering. When we love, we know that the one we love may cause us suffering, but we accept it and are open to it. The greater a love, the greater the suffering it can bear. Paul says it: "Love endures all things" (1 Cor 13:7); this includes suffering. That's how Jesus was: he bore all he did in love for us. The "it is necessary" is the very logic of his love which impelled him from deep within to bear the suffering.

This is all very clear and true as it applies to the human aspect of Jesus' love for us, when we consider Jesus in relation to his humanity, his human love; but what of his divine love for us? This poses a great question, one which has always been controversial and is still not entirely resolved:

can God suffer? For some it is acceptable to say he can, but for others, such as the Greek philosophers, it was not. For the Greeks, it was inadmissible because they viewed suffering as an imperfection, and since God is perfect, he can't suffer. But why say that suffering is an imperfection? Quite the reverse, perfect love undoubtedly bears all things, endures all things, accepts all things, as Paul says (1 Cor 13:7). Why would God in the perfection of his love not suffer? For sure, he doesn't suffer physically, but does he suffer in his heart, in his love, in the fact that he loves?

To the Syriac Fathers, who were not influenced by Greek philosophy, it was clear that God does indeed suffer. We can look at Romanos the Melodist, a Father of the sixth century who was considered a Byzantine but was of Syriac origin and remained profoundly Syriac in his sensibility. In one of his poems, he has God say, "I suffer" (ôdinô, Hymn on Elijah, 24); here, God's suffering is the suffering of his compassion for his people in distress. While the passions are spiritual maladies rooted in sins, compassion is no malady or sin, neither is it an imperfection; it is an expression of love.

We could debate this point endlessly, but wouldn't it be best to ask God himself? What does he say about his suffering? He is very discreet about this, modest and retiring as he is, but there is one place he speaks that can hardly be mistaken, words he spoke one day to Jeremiah in confidence: "Tears roll down from my eyes night and day" (14:17). Jeremiah was able to understand such a confidence from God. These divine tears were not tears of joy but tears of compassion; God suffers because of his people's suffering; the tears are the tears of suffering. God suffers in his compassion through love for his people. As it is with God, it was with Jesus when he wept over Jerusalem (Luke 19:41), over his people with their hearts shut tight. Jesus' tears are both human and divine; they reveal the tears of his Father since the love of Christ is the love of God. Who beside Jesus can reveal the tears of God? The Father and the Son love with the same love and suffer and have compassion with the same love. When the crucified Jesus said, "Father, forgive them because they don't know what they are doing" (Luke 23:34), this means, "Forgive them the sufferings they make me endure and the sufferings they make you endure by crucifying me."

The Septuagint translators understood very well that the tears in Jer 14:17 were indeed God's tears, but they lacked the boldness to translate the verse as it is into Greek because it would have shocked their Greek readers, influenced as they were by Greek philosophy. For this reason they modified the text so that the tears weren't God's but the people's: "Your tears flow from your eyes, night and day!"

It might have shocked the Greeks to think of God shedding tears, but not the Syriacs. Macarius the Great thus also speaks with emotion of God's tears on two occasions in his homilies (1/11 and 30/7).

Yes, God suffers, it is the very logic of his love to endure suffering caused by our sins, our disobedience, our infidelities, by all our failings of love towards him and our brothers and sisters. We cause God the Father, the Son and the Holy Spirit to suffer. Then there is the question of "grieving the Holy Spirit" (Eph 4:30), which also points to suffering, the suffering of sadness we inflict on the Holy Spirit. The tears of sadness are also tears of pain. The Holy Spirit suffers, as do the Father and the Son.

"It is written that the Son of Man will suffer greatly" (9:12)

When Jesus speaks of his suffering, he in fact talks about the suffering of the Son of Man, and so the question arises: what might the Son of Man suffer? There's no doubt that this was also behind Peter's reaction because he knew what is said in the Old Testament about the Son of Man, and knew that nothing is said about his suffering. On this point we do well to listen to a further saying of Jesus which is reported a little later in Mark: "It is written that the Son of Man will suffer greatly" (9:12). The same phrase, "suffer greatly," is used again by Jesus in relation to the Son of Man. On this occasion, when he speaks about the suffering of the Son of Man, he specifies that it is stated in the Scriptures. But what he said isn't actually there! The only text in the Scriptures about the Son of Man is in Daniel (7:13–14), and there is no mention there of suffering. Was Jesus thinking of some other text? Undoubtedly, but which? For centuries the question has been asked, and for centuries it has been considered that Jesus was thinking of Isaiah 53, which tells us of another mysterious personage who endures great suffering and for this reason is often termed "the suffering servant." Neither the expression "suffer greatly" nor indeed "suffer" is there in this text, but everything that is said is full of both physical and inner suffering.

The connection with the Isaiah text is very ancient; it was made in the New Testament in Peter's first letter, which describes Christ in terms of Isaiah 53 (1 Pet 2:21–24). This wonderful text focuses on the suffering of Christ, associating it with the suffering servant.

If then, as Jesus thought, the suffering of the Son of Man had already been announced in the Scriptures, it means that the reality of Christ's suffering had been previewed and announced by God himself, but in a hidden way, no doubt because God is modest and private to the extent of not wishing to clearly state the suffering of his Son; to do so would make him, as Father, suffer too.

In 9:12, Jesus says a little more: "He will suffer greatly and be treated with contempt." The verb here "be treated with contempt"[17] (*exoudénéô*) doesn't reveal physical suffering but profound inner suffering. "Treated with contempt": this is Christ, the Son of Man. "Treated with contempt": it's shocking to hear this on Jesus' lips. He says it in the form of a question which he leaves unanswered: "Why is it written that the Son of Man will suffer greatly and be treated with contempt?" Who is to answer this question?

"Held in contempt": the verb isn't there in Isaiah 53, but the text gets very close to saying it. I don't know who was to reply to Jesus' question, but he knew that Psalm 22 (the psalm of the cross) has a wonderful response which must have warmed his heart: "God has not disdained the prayer of the poor" (22:25 Septuagint)

"It is necessary that he be rejected"

We return now to the first announcement of the Passion. "It is necessary that he be rejected": the verb here (*apodokimazô*) again expresses suffering for the Son of Man. Jesus specifies that he will be "rejected by the elders, the chief priests and the scribes," and this comes to pass in the account of the Passion. The verb "reject" is not used in the Passion story, but the idea is the same, though a different verb is used: the soldiers "mock" him (*empaïzô*, 15:20), as do the people's leaders (15:31). Perhaps it was bearable that the soldiers would mock him, but it is more painful

17. The French would be translated literally as "regarded as nothing," which is "set at nought" in the KJV. "Treated with contempt" is frequent in English translations, for example the AMP.

that the leaders should mock and reject him because these leaders were the religious leaders, the spiritual authorities. That's very hard: the people who cause Jesus the most suffering were the representatives of God, men of God. But what suffering for God too to see his representatives making his Son suffer. And what love was needed from Christ, what a power of love to say to his Father, "Father, forgive them, they don't know what they are doing," as Luke tells us (23:34).

Apodokimazôi is found in just one other place in Mark, in a passage of great interest in which Jesus quotes the Scriptures: "The stone which the builders rejected is become the cornerstone" (Ps 118:22 in Mark 12:10). Jesus uses this quotation at the close of the parable of the vine-dressers which announces the death and resurrection of the well-beloved son, that is, Christ. The quotation shows that Jesus self-identified as this stone "rejected" by the religious leaders whom God honors by making him the chief cornerstone of his building. We notice that Jesus had read in the Scriptures, in this psalm, the announcement by which he would live. Very discreetly, the cross was announced in the Old Testament. Without the help of the Holy Spirit, such a reading of the psalm was surely impossible, so we find that it's through the Holy Spirit that the Son could read in the Scriptures what the Father would do to honor him. It's extraordinary for us to be able here to approach to some degree the experience of the Son with the Holy Spirit before the Father, and we thus, to some degree, approach the mystery of the Trinity.

"It is necessary that he be killed"

"It is necessary that he be killed"; the verb "to kill" (*apokteinô*) is very violent, indeed too violent for a disciple to hear; no wonder Peter reacted. It was unacceptable that the Christ be killed. No messianic prophecy announced the death of the Messiah, as indeed the crowd witnesses in John's gospel: "We have learned in the law that the Christ remains eternally" (12:34). This is the Messiah, the Christ, who Peter had just been confessing. If Jesus was the Christ, as Peter thought, then it was insupportable and revolting to hear Jesus announce his death. It was even more insupportable that the death be presented by Jesus as a murder. Peter wasn't rebelling without cause.

It's true that Jesus doesn't speak here of the Christ but of the Son of Man, but let's not play with words; Peter had correctly understood that Jesus is the Son of Man. At all events, no Scriptural text announces the death of the Son of Man. Jesus' statement was just unacceptable.

By announcing that he would be killed, Jesus was denouncing a plot that was being prepared of which Peter was completely unaware. The plot had already been suggested by Mark after the healing of the man with the withered hand: "The Pharisees went out and immediately consulted with the Herodians how to destroy him" (3:6). The plot was being prepared in great secrecy, and Peter knew nothing of it.

The plot would come to fruition as we see early in the Passion account, where Mark takes up the word "kill" again: "The feast of Passover and the unleavened bread was to take place in two days time; the chief priests and the scribes sought how to arrest Jesus by trickery and kill him" (14:1). Mark's gospel is carefully constructed; Peter can have known nothing about this.

"To be killed": Peter might have particularly reacted to this because the verb is passive, and it could well have been a divine passive, leaving the unacceptable to be understood, that Jesus would be killed by God! Of course, the Passion account says the reverse (14:1), that it was men who would kill Jesus, not God; the parable of the vinedressers makes this more specific, where we find the verb "kill" with the vinedressers as the subject, killing the son (12:7–8).

In the same way, Jesus is clear in this announcement of the Passion; his use of the passive verb does not have God as its agent but men: "He will be rejected by the elders, the chief priests and the scribes"; this leaves it as understood that it is they who will kill the Christ. While this is true, the passive about being killed is not so precise, so we might still think of it as a divine passive. It's therefore not impossible that Peter might have understood Christ being put to death as a divine passive; the doubt might have been sown.

The remainder of Jesus' statement announces his resurrection, which would have reassured Peter, though even this is not so clear when we learn that shortly afterwards the disciples "were asking what rising from the dead meant" (9:10).

Peter's reaction shows that Jesus would have to tackle the subject again, which indeed he did in order to remove the misunderstandings and make things clearer.

"It is necessary that he rise"

"It is necessary that he rise": the disciples had difficulty understanding this, Mark tells us a little further on (9:10). This incomprehension is astonishing because the disciples knew that the Old Testament clearly affirmed people being raised. The son of the widow at Zarapheth was certainly raised[18] in the time of the prophet Elijah (1 Kgs 17:17–24),

18. There are always two words used in French, *resurrection* as a noun and *ressusciter* as a verb. Where English uses resurrection to speak only of Jesus and of the resurrection on the last day, French uses *resurrection* as the noun for being raised, as here.

as well as the Shunamite's son in the time of Elisha (2 Kgs 4:32–37). So why didn't the disciples understand?

"To rise": [19] the verb used by Jesus here, *anistèmi*, means firstly "to raise oneself." Here it is active, not passive, which is important and surprising because it means that Jesus wasn't saying that he would be resuscitated, raised from among the dead, by his Father, but that he would raise himself, on his own; in other words, that he would resuscitate himself. What could be more extraordinary! In Jesus' time, the Pharisees believed in the resurrection, which is to say they believed that God was able to give life back to the dead. This was admitted, but no one said that a person could raise themselves, and it is this that Jesus affirms here. With this in mind, I understand why Mark tells us that the disciples were asking what it meant to "rise from the dead" (9:10, the same verb *anistèmi*, always active). This comment from Mark comes at the moment Jesus repeats that the Son of Man "will rise[20] from the dead" (9:9, the same verb in the active form). As John Chrysostom says: "It is an extraordinary and indeed strange thing that a man should resuscitate himself" (*Homilies on Saint John's gospel*, 23/3).[21] In John's gospel, another statement of Jesus' is recorded, spelling out Jesus' announcement that he would raise himself: "In three days, I will raise the Temple," which means that he himself would raise his own body (2:19–21).

This is, however, exactly what Jesus announced, and it was bound to shock the disciples: he told them that he

19. Literally, "to resuscitate."

20. Raise himself. The French is a reflexive verb. In French you don't, for example, simply "wash"; you "wash yourself," the reflexive form.

21. The reflexive idea, present in the French, is also present in the Greek. Our English is lacking.

would raise himself! There were reasons for their incomprehension. However, what could show more clearly that he is God!

Perhaps it was a lack of humility to teach such a thing? We might think so, but we mustn't forget that Jesus was hiding behind the figure of the Son of Man, and it is humility that led him to do this. I believe mainly that in daring to speak in this way, Jesus was strengthening the disciples, who must have been shaken by all they had been hearing about the suffering and death of the Son of Man, a word so difficult to receive that Peter for one resisted it vigorously. It was love for his disciples that led Jesus to announce his resurrection here; it was encouraging, comforting and reassuring.

However, reader friend, another statement of Jesus will surprise us further; the evening before his death, Jesus told his disciples something quite different and spoke of his resurrection not with an active verb but with a different and passive verb (égeïrô): "After I am raised, I will go ahead of you to Galilee" (14:28). The passive of the verb here could only be a divine passive and so gives it to be understood that Jesus would be raised by God, his Father. This is exactly what the angel announced to the women on Easter morning: "He has been raised" (égeïô in the passive, 16:6). What are we to understand now? Was Jesus raised by himself or by his Father?

In fact, any contradiction is no more than apparent; there is in reality a paradox which arises from stating two truths about the same thing, that Jesus would raise himself and that he would be raised by his Father. The two statements are to be held together, teaching us that Easter is the mutual work of the Father and the Son. This is doubtless why the resurrection of Jesus is not described; it's beyond our understanding that Jesus should raise himself at the same time as being raised by his Father! The great mystery of Easter is right here in this mutual work of the Father and the Son.

That there is a paradox in expressing the resurrection of Christ is inevitable given the limitations of language. There is no voice in Greek or our modern languages which can express both active and passive at the same time; it just doesn't exist. This being so, a paradox is the only possibility if we are to express both when we know that we have to make both statements. With the disciples, Jesus uses the active here and later the passive, not to state two contradictory truths but one which can't otherwise be expressed: the resurrection of Christ is a mutual work of the Father and the Son. This paradox immerses us again in the silence of contemplating the Risen One.

To indicate the extent to which his resurrection is beyond description, Jesus uses two verbs when he speaks of it, *anistèmi* (8:41) and égeïrô (14:28); neither of the two alone manages to state the reality which is beyond both; each of them only approaches the truth; we need a third term which would contain them both, but there is none. The resurrection of Christ is inexpressible, a wonderful, profound mystery which we can but contemplate.

The second announcement of the Passion (Mark 9:31–32)

31. He taught his disciples, saying, "The Son of Man is delivered into the hands of men; they will kill him, and three days after being killed, he will rise." 32. They didn't understand this and were afraid to ask.

Jesus' first teaching on the Passion was so difficult both to give and receive that Jesus needed to repeat it, and that is what he does here, where we find the verb "teach" with

Jesus as its subject and the disciples the recipients. Jesus always spoke to them not of himself but of the Son of Man, with modesty and delicacy to avoid shocking the disciples. But the result was the same: the disciples failed to understand. Jesus therefore had to engage the subject again.

This second statement is astonishing: Jesus is even more brief. He had already been brief in 8:31, but here he is more so. This great concision seems to me to be the sign of Jesus being troubled, of great emotion; we can understand because the theme is the same: "The Son of Man is delivered into the hands of men; they will kill him and three days after being killed, he will rise."

There is nothing new here specifically about the resurrection: it is announced as in 8:31. We can, however, point to two new pieces of information. One is a necessary and welcome precision. The preceding teaching in fact left some doubt whether it was God who would cause the Son of Man to die, but Jesus clears this up: it was not God but men who would kill him. Jesus doesn't insist or specify which men. With no superfluous word, the guilty party is stated but in general terms. Jesus discreetly says nothing more.

What is entirely new here is the use of the verb "deliver," which we need to examine since it is a word that recurs in the account of the Passion; it is there ten times in chapters 14 and 15. We are told that Judas delivered Jesus to the religious leaders (14:10), that they delivered him to Pilate (15:1), and that he then delivered him to the cross (15:15). It's this that filled Jesus with emotion and caused him to speak so concisely.

"The Son of Man is delivered"

"The Son of Man is delivered": Jesus here uses the verb "deliver" in the passive, without specifying by whom he will be delivered. It is this silence which reveals Jesus' emotion. Who was going to deliver him, to hand him over? The principal subject of the verb in the Passion account is Judas (14:10, 11, 18, 21, 41, 42, 44). From the opening of the gospel, Judas is presented as the one who will hand Jesus over (3:19), and Judas was now present among the disciples Jesus was addressing. Nothing further is said of his intentions, so we don't know if the project was already in his mind; but if we don't know, Jesus must already have known because he knew his disciple's heart. It seems to me that this is enough to explain Jesus' silence. His delicacy led Jesus not to name the one who would deliver him. We understand this, but it's not all.

The passive verb might well be a divine passive, which would lead us to think that it is was God who was going to hand over the Son of Man. This might also explain Jesus' silence very well. It would have been too difficult for him to say — difficult for Jesus to say and difficult for the disciples to hear. Jesus preferred to keep quiet. Nevertheless, he gave an important detail which might reveal that the passive is indeed a divine passive: "He is delivered into the hands of men." The word "men" in the plural fits better with the meaning of God handing him over to men rather than of Judas delivering him to the religious leaders.

To this can be added the fact the Jesus uses the word "deliver" in the present. If Jesus was thinking of Judas, he would have used the future ("The Son of Man will be delivered"), the same future as the rest of the statement. In fact, Judas had not yet handed him over. In contrast, if Jesus thought that God was handing him over, then the present tense fits since in the heart of God the Son of Man had already been handed over. But what a revolution of thought if the Son of Man was handed over to man by God, if Jesus was delivered over by his Father!

Tell me, is it possible that God would hand over his Son? Is or is not the passive used by Jesus really a divine passive? Well, yes! What Jesus is leaving to be understood is clearly stated by Paul in his letter to the Romans: "God did not spare his Son and handed him over for us all" (8:32). This statement has something brutal about it, but it is clear. It may shock us, but we should realize that it is a counterpoint to another statement that is inseparable from it, even though it's in another letter: "Christ handed himself over for me" (Gal 2:20). Before going further, we need to put these two statements together.

Paul affirms on one hand that God handed over his Son, and, on the other, that his Son delivered himself. This is very important! It demonstrates full agreement between the Father and the Son. To understand this properly, we need to think in terms of the Trinity, in which the three divine persons have one and the same will, one and the same goal. We have already discussed this, and it is confirmed here; what the Father thinks and wants is what the Son thinks and wants. Neither imposes anything on the other. They are one with the Holy Spirit, beyond our understanding: a perfect, inseparable unity. If we put aside the divinity of Christ in our reading of these verses, if Jesus was no more than a man, then we might indeed rebel as did Peter. But we know who it is that motivates rebellion against the things of God: Satan. It's therefore clear for Paul, and I hope for you too: the Father handed over his Son, who is also God; and the Son handed himself over, in perfect harmony. Once again, if Jesus was no more than a man, then God is a sadistic, perverse god.

This becomes even clearer when Paul teaches us why the Son was delivered up by both himself and his Father. Paul says this very clearly. In the passage from the letter to the Romans where we are told that the Father hands over the Son, Paul immediately develops his argument into the verses that wonderfully say that nothing, absolutely nothing, can separate us from the love God has manifested to us in Jesus Christ (8:38–39). It was in love for us that God handed over his Son. If this is still too hard for us to welcome into our hearts, we can then listen to Paul tell us again why Christ handed over himself. He tells the Galatians, "Christ loved me, he gave himself for me" (2:20). This is the only verse in which Paul talks about the love of Jesus for him. He was overwhelmed as he wrote this, and it might well overwhelm us too. This makes still more evident the depth of the cross: Jesus handed himself over out of love for Paul as he did for each of us, for me, for you . . .

Uniting the Father and the Son most deeply is their love for us. The Father hands over the Son out of love for us, and the Son hands himself over out of love for us. There is this unfathomable depth in the communion of love of the Father and the Son for us; at once a universal love for us all collectively (Rom 8), and a personal love for each of us (Gal 2). How utterly wonderful!

The third announcement of the Passion (Mark 10:32–45)

32. As they were on their way, going up to Jerusalem, Jesus went ahead of them and they were troubled and afraid as they followed him. He took the Twelve again and began to tell them what was going to happen to him: 33. "We're going up to Jerusalem; the Son of Man will be handed over to the chief priests and scribes; they will condemn him to death and deliver him to the Gentiles; 34. they will mock him, spit on him, scourge him and kill him; three days later he will rise."[. . .]

45. The Son of Man did not come to be served but to serve and to give his life as a ransom for many."

This third announcement of the Passion is again spoken by Jesus to the disciples, on this occasion as they are going to Jerusalem. It was interrupted, not this time by Peter but by James and John, who by their intervention (vv 35–44) show us that again they had not understood, their pride in the way; even the other disciples were indignant at this. Jesus rebukes James and John and concludes with a verse of great importance for our understanding of the cross, verse 45.

In this third announcement, Jesus focuses again on the Son of Man. This is clear, but Mark has an odd way of introducing it; he tells us that Jesus "took the Twelve again and began to tell them what was going to happen to him." "What was going to happen to *him*," to *him*, that is Jesus; but the continuation doesn't talk about him but about the Son of Man. This elision of Jesus and the Son of Man discreetly but clearly reveals that Jesus is the Son of Man.

There is practically nothing new here. The word for "deliver" or "hand over" is used firstly in the passive but this time in the future rather than the present, giving us to understand that the Son of Man will be handed over not by God but by Judas, who indeed delivered him to the chief priests and scribes (14:10); then it is used a second time in the future but with an active meaning, signifying that these last would hand him over to the Gentiles. There's nothing more: Jesus doesn't here talk about the mystery of God's love and limits himself to announcing events on the basic human level, that is, the plot fomented against him by men.

The only additions here are the details about the suffering to be inflicted on Jesus by the Gentiles: physical sufferings, that he would be scourged; and moral sufferings, being mocked and spat upon. What can I say about these painful details? Nothing! Only the silence of our compassion has any place here, together with our repentance.

What is new is the final verse, following the interruption of James and John. Jesus says, "The Son of Man did not come to be served but to serve and to give his life as a ransom for many." This most important verse merits our full attention.

"To give his life"

"To give his life": that means to die, but it points to how. Not all deaths are the same. Some are very honorable and others not. People can die guilty or innocent, surrounded by friends or abandoned, gloriously or in degradation. To give one's life; this is to be generous, to give freely, and is generally considered very positive, even noble.

Hearing that Jesus would give his life, the disciples must have felt a real sense of relief: they weren't going to take Jesus' life by killing him, he was going to give it himself freely, of his own will. "No one takes my life from me, I give it," Jesus said in in John' gospel, using different terms (10:18). In Jesus' eyes, it was not a murder being perpetrated against him but an offering ripening in his heart. I believe the relief the disciples felt is apparent in the silence that followed. Mark, in fact, stops his account here; immediately after this statement of Jesus, the disciples say nothing further. This was a first: after the first announcement, Peter rebelled; after the second, Mark says that the disciples hadn't understood and were afraid to ask Jesus. This time, Mark doesn't report any reaction from the disciples. Their silence seems to me be a silence, if rather unsure, of relief. It remained to be seen how Jesus would give his life. The disciples knew nothing of this yet; the unfolding of events would let them know.

"He came"

"He came": Jesus speaks of the gift of his life in a very positive way. "The Son of Man came for this." The use of the verb "come" has a very precise meaning in the biblical context. The verb means that this "coming" was to accomplish a mission received from God. The verb is found right at the beginning of the gospel when John the Baptist announces the coming of Jesus: "He is coming, one who is mightier than me" (1:27). In saying this, John the Baptist was announcing an emissary from God. "Come" in this context means come from beside God. The verb is later on the Baptist's lips when he asks Jesus, "Are you the one who is to come?" (Matt 11:3). Most commonly the verb is applied to the Messiah (cf John 4:25: "I know that the Messiah must come," says the Samaritan woman to Jesus. Here, Jesus employs the term for the Son of Man as he states the essence of his mission: "He came to give his life." Thus enlightened by Jesus, the disciples would have understood that Jesus had come from God to give his life. If God had entrusted this mission to him, it could only be positive. Every mission entrusted by God is positive.

This mission has a surprising aspect, that after the three first announcements which contained the terrible word "kill," which is used twice in the third announcement, Jesus suddenly states something quite different, "give his life."

With this, Jesus' death appears in a very different light. Until this point, Jesus had spoken of it as the result of a plot fomented by men, while now he speaks of it as something written into the plan of God. At first glance, if we look at the surface reality, Jesus' death was indeed a human plot being pursued to its end; looked at in depth, in the depths of God's heart, it's something very different, a blessing from God.

Into the murder there comes the idea of an offering!

The two ways of looking at the cross are both correct. What men were to do by crucifying Jesus is manifestly very negative, even vile and revolting. However, God in his project of love transforms this evil into good, unbeknownst to the plotters. It was the same with Joseph the patriarch, sold by his brothers: God turned back the evil they committed in such a way that later Joseph would say to them, "You thought to do me evil, but God has changed it into good" (Gen 50:20). This could also be said about the cross. Those who plotted against Jesus and crucified him knew nothing about it, but God positively transformed the cross by the offering of the Crucified One. Those who crucified Jesus were, so to speak, used without their knowing it by God in order for the offering to take place.

This transformation of the situation would be repeated and confirmed by Jesus in the parable he devoted to this subject, the parable of the vinedressers, who plotted and put to death the well-beloved son; but the Father comes to raise his son, to make this stone rejected by men the headstone of his building (12:1–12). We can marvel along with the psalm cited by Jesus at the end of the parable as we see that this all comes from God: "It is marvelous in our eyes" (12:11, quoting Ps 118:23).

This also sheds light, I believe, on the "it is necessary" of the first announcement: it is necessary that he be put to death because this enables the Son of Man to accomplish his mission and give his life with inexpressible love.

After such an unexpected new vista, Mark says nothing more; he lifts his pen and contemplates what has been announced: Jesus will give his life . . .

The disciples too were deep in silence.

"To serve"

Jesus also describes his mission as service: "He did not come to be served but to serve." The verb "serve" (*diakonéô*) used here is a little different from another term (*douleuô*) which is more widely used in the Bible. *Douleuô* qualifies a service which most often is constrained, obligated or paid; the word for slavery (*douléïai*) derives from it. In apposition to this, *daikonéô* designates a freely given, benevolent, voluntary service given gratuitously; from it comes our word deacon (*diakonos*, Acts 6:1–6), which Mark's Roman readers knew very well, as they had deacons in their community.

By using *diakonéô*, Jesus defines his mission as a voluntary, free service that had nothing imposed or constrained about it. This means that he himself adhered fully to his mission with total liberty. This was the Son's relation to the Father and to us. If he was giving his life, it was fully of his own will in a generous outpouring of his heart. He was giving it as a voluntary offering.

At the same time, this service was being given by Christ in the most total humility because the Son of Man makes himself a servant of all to whom he was giving his life. The silence of the disciples as they heard this was beyond words. They must have seen Jesus in a radically new aspect. This is the first and only time that Jesus designates himself as a servant in Mark's gospel. It was a revelation he was giving them. The disciples had a servant before them; they had never seen Jesus in this light, he who was the glorious

Son of Man of Daniel's vision. They were discovering this and were silent as they contemplated him in a different light than they had before . . .

The ransom (*lutron*)

There remains one word to examine, a word that is unique to Mark's gospel in the sense that it is not taken up in the gospels of Luke and John, and is only found in the parallel verse in Matthew (20:28); this is the word "ransom," *lutron*, which derives from the verb *lutroô* which means "deliver," "set free."

The difficulty with the word is that Jesus doesn't comment or accompany it with anything that might help us understand. "To give his life as a ransom," very surely means that the life of Jesus will permit others to be freed from their slavery. Jesus' humble service is for the benefit of those who would thus by freed thanks to him. This much is clear, but there are questions that arise. Who would be freed and from what slavery? If there is a ransom, to whom was the ransom to be paid? There are so many questions that Jesus didn't answer but which nevertheless impose themselves on us and no doubt on the disciples too. Their silence would therefore be somewhat questioning. What exactly was Jesus saying?

The first question to tackle is to whom the ransom was to be paid. Who would claim the ransom or require it for the slaves to go free? Very quickly the Church Fathers applied themselves to this question, and they were divided: some thought the life of Jesus was a price due to his Father who therefore required Jesus' death; others, that Satan required the ransom. The division lasted until the time of Gregory the Nazarene (in the 4th century), who said that the Bible supported neither meaning and simply ignored the question.

To see in God a Father who demands the ransom of his Son doesn't fit at all; God is not perverse. And if Satan sought such a ransom, it would do him far too much honor to respond to such a demand. Jesus wasn't offering his life to Satan. Gregory suggested that the question was a false one, to be ignored, since it just takes us away from the meaning of the image. Jesus said, "to give his life as a ransom *for* many," not, "give his life a ransom to so-and-so." If we listen to Jesus carefully, the real question is not to whom the ransom was payable, but for whom, in favor of whom; the ancillary question has to do with the nature of the slavery from which people were to be freed. To this question, the Bible does have an answer.

Even though certain commentators have not listened to Gregory and have continued to speculate in vain, we will put aside what is in effect an unreal question.

"To give his life a ransom for many": the word "many" must certainly refer to people; on this point the unanimity of commentators is a given: it is indeed people for whom Jesus gives his life, but it remains for us to specify the exact meaning of "many."

Before doing this, we need to understand first the slavery from which the ransomed are to be freed. The disciples were right to question among themselves; the deliverance might have been political as much as spiritual. The ambiguity the disciples were left with helps us understand why the disciples on the way to Emmaus thought in terms of a political deliverance, of deliverance from Roman oppression: "We hoped that it would be he that would liberate Israel" (Luke 24:21, with the verb *lutroô* from which *lutron* derives). No doubt, Judas had also understood Jesus' mission as political. We mustn't judge them; the indefinite character of Jesus' statement might have left them with this understanding.

Between the moment Jesus spoke to the disciples and the moment Mark began to write his gospel, a good thirty years had passed. When the Christians in Rome read the gospel, they had benefited from the teaching of Peter and Paul. For the question that concerns us here, it is Paul who is most useful, pronouncing as he does on the meaning of the deliverance obtained by Christ. He didn't do so leaning on his own intuition but following meditation in the Scriptures.

The Scriptures do speak of political deliverance as well as spiritual. The Old Testament speaks at length about the deliverances from oppression in Egypt (Exod 6:6; 15:13) and Babylon (Jer 31:11.)[22] Here, the political deliverance comes from God through the intervention of his envoys, Moses and Cyrus (his anointed).[23] The Old Testament also speaks of deliverance from sin (Ps 130:8) and from death (Hos 13:14), and in these cases, God alone, without any representative, is responsible for the deliverance: "I will deliver (*lutroô*) them from death," says God in Hos 13;14. "It is the Lord who delivers (*lutroô*) Israel from all his iniquities" (Ps 130:8). Paul definitely needed to be led by the Holy Spirit in his choice between the two types of deliverance.

Paul resolutely favors the spiritual meaning, meaning that for him, Jesus came to deliver from the slavery of sin and death. This being so, it follows that in setting us free Jesus was not an envoy or representative of God but God himself since God has no need of any helper to free people from sin and death. It's because Jesus is God that his death is deliverance from sin and death. No person, however

22. "The Lord has redeemed Jacob and ransomed him from the hand of him that was stronger than he."

23. Fr. *Cyrus ou le Messie.* Literally, Cyrus or the Messiah. see Is 45.1.

extraordinary, could by death free others from sin and death. Moreover, no man by his death has ever freed others from sin and death.

I would point to a particularly clear verse from Paul in his letter to Titus: "Our great God and Savior Jesus Christ gave himself to deliver (*lutroô*) us from all iniquity" (2:14). This is wonderfully said. With the mention of "all iniquity," Paul's phrase clearly gives the meaning of a spiritual deliverance wrought by Jesus on the cross. "To give oneself" is "to give one's life." We also find in the Greek *uper*, meaning "in favor of or for," alongside the verb *lutroô*. Clearly, Jesus delivers us not from Roman oppression but from iniquity.

Paul was inspired by the verse from the Psalm that says, "It is the Lord who delivers Israel from all his iniquities" (130:8). Paul must have meditated this verse at length to conclude that the Lord God of whom the psalm speaks is none other than Jesus in his divinity. To underline the divinity of Christ, Paul terms Jesus "Our great God and Savior." "Our great God and Savior Jesus Christ": Paul could not be more explicit about the divinity of Jesus!

Not only does Jesus deliver us from our sins, our iniquities, as Paul says along with the psalm, but his gift had to be total and extend to delivering us from death which is the consequence of sin (Rom 6:23). To deliver us from death, death itself had to be confronted and vanquished. This is what Jesus did. The prophecy of Hosea had announced this when reporting the word of God: "I will deliver (*lutroô*) you from death" (13:14). Paul specifies this by speaking of death as an "enemy" to which we are slaves, saying that "the last enemy to be destroyed is death" (1 Cor 15:26). As with Hosea's prophecy (13:14), for Paul this victory remained in the future but is attributed to Christ.

But how could the death of a man "destroy" death, according to the term used by Paul (*katargéô*, to abrogate, annul, abolish)? What power could be stronger than death? I see only one: love; but it matters whose love. Human love is not strong enough. The Song of Songs well says that "love is strong as death" (8:6). Not "stronger" but "as strong," equally. This is true of human love but not divine love, which alone is stronger than death. Jesus is overflowing with love, but if he was merely a man, his love, extraordinary as it is, would not be victorious over death. On the contrary, because he is God, his love, which is an inexpressible love beyond any other, this infinite love of which John is the singer and Mark its contemplative, this love is enough to destroy death. I thus understand that it was necessary for Jesus to give his life with the divine love which is his. It was necessary too that he pursue incarnation to its very end, to the point of giving, of giving his life, to dying, in order to conquer death. The first sign of his victory was given us on Easter morning.

For many or for all?

Just who will be set free by the life of Jesus given as a ransom?

While Jesus speaks of a ransom "for many," Paul writes to Titus that it was "for us." Of whom was Paul speaking? Of "us," the Christians; or of "us," men and women? The question might arise, but no longer stands when we read what Paul wrote to Timothy: "Jesus Christ gave himself a ransom *for all*" (1 Tim 2:6). He says this in a passage where he has just specified that "God wants all people to be saved" (2:4). In this sense, for Paul, the death of Christ was clearly for all people. But if this is so, why did Jesus speak of "many" rather than "all"?

The word *polloï* translated as "many" can also mean "a multitude," which clarifies the reach of the term; nevertheless, while the gap between "a multitude" and "all people" is a little less, there is still a gap.

I would find it very difficult to say that Paul misrepresented the teaching of his Lord; on the contrary, I find the humility of Jesus to be magnificent as he presents himself not as one whose mission is universal but as one who puts himself at the service of "many," without venturing to say it was in service of "all." Nonetheless, in the vision of Daniel, the Son of Man appears above the whole earth, and it is said of him that "he was given sovereignty, glory and royalty; and all peoples, nations and individuals of all tongues will serve him" (7:14). The Son of Man here has a universal stature. It was in humility that Jesus said simply "many." He doubtless wished to remain with the perspective of the humble suffering servant of whom it is said that "he bore the sins of many people" (Is 53:12). In doing so, it seems to me, Jesus wonderfully brings together the figure of the Son of Man and the suffering servant. Without wishing to misrepresent the humility of Jesus, I believe with Paul that the mission of Christ was to offer his life on the cross for the salvation of all people. "Many" might also mean "from humanity, all those who accept becoming beneficiaries of the ransom given by Christ"; this is a way of respecting the liberty of all.

What else is there to say about the distance between "many" and "all"? My belief is that pedagogically this is very positive for us. What am I saying? If we adhere solely to the deliverance of all people through the cross, we might be tempted into negligence. Indeed, if we know that we are saved through the death of Christ, there is a risk of our considering this salvation as so thoroughly acquired that we begin to live without caring, in total negligence. There would be no need to care about anything given that we are already saved. Such negligence can then draw us into worse excesses and far from Christ. On the other hand, if the deliverance from sin and death has been obtained not for all but for many, then our desire for salvation will guard us against negligence and call us to do all in our power to belong to the "many" of whom Jesus speaks. However, we then risk falling into the trap of spiritual activism with a view to a salvation obtained by our works and not by grace.

Is it therefore necessary to choose between the salvation of all by grace or of the many by works? No. We need to keep the two truths as elements of a paradox that points to the inexpressible salvation obtained by Christ, beyond the healthy tension between "many" and "all."

After listening to these announcements of the Passion, I am struck that none of them is addressed directly to the disciples in terms of how they might concern and affect them. Jesus progressively makes clearer the meaning of his death, bringing us little by little into the mystery of the offering of his life. Even as he hides behind the figure of the Son of Man, not saying "I" so as to avoid being overcome by the emotion speaking of his own death would entail, he also maintains a distance from the disciples, without implicating them in any way. Not once, in fact, in these announcements does he say "you," as he speaks to the disciples; again, it seems to me, as a way of sheltering them from excessive emotion.

We can nevertheless feel that he is very close to addressing them directly. Perhaps this is why he says nothing more even though not everything had been said. He stops on this vague word, "many," giving his life for "many." I believe he stops speaking at the very moment he might have said just what his feelings stopped him from saying: "Giving his life for many, including you, my disciples, to deliver you too from death, to deliver you too from your sins. It is for you, my children (10:24), that I make the offering of my life, freely. It is for you that I make myself a servant, your servant. I came for this, to give my life, to free you from your denials and betrayals, to deliver you too, Peter, and you, Judas . . ."

But no! In his great reserve and modesty, in his unfathomable humility, Jesus contents himself with saying that "the Son of Man is come to give his life a ransom for many." He goes no further, preferring to be silent. But what infinite love there is in the silence . . .

After hearing Jesus announce his death to them, the disciples were silent too. Jesus had no need to speak further; each knew himself involved; each understood that it was for him that Jesus was giving his life.

None of them said a word.

In silence they followed Jesus as he passed through Jericho on his way up to Jerusalem. Here began the way of the cross . . .

Lord Jesus,
I believe that one day I will find myself before you and the
    Father
and that then you will fix your gaze on me.
I know that you will be ready to tell me,
"It's for you that I gave my life";
but I believe you so modest and humble
that in your emotion you won't manage to say it.
It will be enough that you invite me to raise my eyes to yours,
and I know that in your eyes all your love will be revealed.
Eternity will then unfold in silence.
I can stay there, unmoving.
Eternity will not be enough.
There will be no more reason for words
for no words could ever tell the depth of your love.
How true; it's beyond words in the depth of the deeps.
And now, today, Lord, I begin in this silence.
I believe you've given your life for me;
I'm overwhelmed and fall down,
my heart full of thanksgiving.
Today, I have no need to see you face to face;
it's not yet time.
I am still too blinded by my sin
and tears of repentance prevent me from seeing you.
May the Holy Spirit pursue his work in my heart;
May today, now, he help me prepare a little.
May he come to cleanse my heart and purify me
that in the last day I may stand before you in silence,
with eyes still filled with tears.
Then you will wipe the tears away and I will be able to
    contemplate you . . .

I bless you, you who give us a love I cannot tell,
you who live and reign with the Father and the Holy Spirit
now and always and throughout the ages. Amen.

THE TRANSFIGURATION

(MARK 9:2–8)

2. Six days later, Jesus took with him Peter, James and John and led them up into a high mountain, apart and by themselves; and he was transfigured before them. 3. His garments became shining white, whiter than any earthly laundering could make them. 4. Elijah appeared to them with Moses, and they conversed with Jesus. 5. Peter spoke up, saying to Jesus, "Rabbi, it is good that we are here with you; let us make three tents, one for you, one for Moses and one for Elijah." 6. This was because he didn't know what to say because they were gripped by great fear. 7. Then there came a cloud, covering them with its shadow, and there came a voice from the cloud, "This is my beloved Son. Hear him!" 8. Immediately, when they looked around they saw no one but Jesus there with them.

"Six days later"

"SIX DAYS LATER": AFTER WHAT? MARK DID NOT CUSTOMarily locate events in relation to each other. That he does so here is to invite us to put this account alongside the one that precedes it, which is to say, the words Jesus had recently spoken to his hearers: "Amen, I tell you that among those here some will not taste death before they see the Kingdom of God come with power" (9:1).

This is the announcement of a very solemn event, the coming of the Kingdom of God. Could anyone other than a prophet announce the coming of the Kingdom? A prophet would be expected, but here Jesus makes a prophetic announcement without using a prophetic formula. The most frequently used formula to introduce a prophecy was "thus says the Lord God" (Amos 1:3,6, 9 . . .). The formula enabled a prophet to introduce a Word from God that they had been charged with announcing. The surprising feature here, as we have noted, is that Jesus didn't say "the Lord God says," but "I say," demonstrating an authority superior to a prophet's.

"I tell you": Jesus introduces this authority filled formula with the word "Amen," which means "in truth." "Amen, I tell you": this turn of phrase is typical of Jesus' discourse, in Mark as well as in the other gospels. No one other than him speaks like this anywhere in the Bible because, in the biblical tradition, the word "Amen" is always a final word, the close of a talk (2 Pet 3:18), the response given by a person or an assembly to someone who has been speaking to indicate full assent, full agreement (Rev 5:14); Jesus is the first and only one to use this word not as a conclusion but as an introduction; not at the close of a discourse or phrase but at the outset, as if he wished to take over from human speech and speak of things never spoken before, with an astonishing authority.

"Amen, I tell you": never had anyone spoken like this; never had anyone dared to set themselves above the prophets, which would be to take oneself for God. That Jesus would do so was either a sign of blasphemous pride or that that he is simply God. If he is God, we can understand with what authority he said what he did. This manner of speech imparts to the words that follow an immense importance, the importance of speech from God. What is being announced is indeed from God: the coming of the Kingdom of God.

If we hold on to the conclusive sense of "Amen," as a brother suggested to me, we can think that by saying "Amen" Jesus is affirming something the Father had said to him in private talk, and was closing their conversation before passing on its conclusions. Thus, we might understand here: "Amen! I tell you now what my Father has told me concerning the coming of the Kingdom." Wonderful!

The event six days later was precisely the transfiguration. Is there a difference between the announcement (of the Kingdom of God) and the event (the transfiguration)? It's not for us to judge. At all events, the disciples had understood Jesus' announcement and they were sure that the Kingdom of God was on the way.

"To see the Kingdom of God come with power": what was this power of which Jesus speaks? Perhaps a military power with an armed force? We know very well it's not so. So what is this power? If I have understood the Gospel correctly, and if you have too, the issue here is the power of divine love; this power is completely real and extraordinary, but of quite a different order to the power of an army.

What does "the Kingdom of God" on Jesus' lips mean? It is this we will uncover in the account of the transfiguration.

"Before *seeing* the Kingdom come," Jesus says: what he is announcing will be visible, which effectively happens in our passage; the verb "see" is used, and the description is highly visual. Then Jesus specifies that it will only be seen be "some of those here," which again, comes to pass; only Peter, James and John would be witnesses to the transfiguration.

What happened during the preceding six days of which Mark speaks? Mark is silent about it, but we can suppose that what took place is what would take place in the hearts of men awaiting the coming of the Kingdom of God. We can imagine them over the space of these six days with their hearts in a somewhat frenzied enthusiasm but also in deep repentance. If God is indeed coming, it is essential to open oneself up to him in prayer, in repentance, setting the heart in order where it is disordered. This is all the more true in that Jesus calls us from the beginning of his ministry to "repent because the Kingdom of God is at hand" (1:15).

"Six days later, Jesus took with him Peter, James and John," the same three disciples he had taken to be witnesses of another extraordinary act, the raising of Jairus' daughter (5:37). No doubt these three disciples were to be witnesses of something just as extraordinary, if not more so. It would seem that the more out of the ordinary an event, the fewer witnesses Jesus wanted with him. This was doubtless dictated by his humility.

"He led them up"

"He led them up": the verb used by Mark here is difficult to translate. *Anaphérô* means "cause to climb," or, more precisely, "carry upwards": so, Jesus carried or bore the three disciples upwards! What is this saying?

Of course, Mark wasn't saying that Jesus carried the three disciples on his back to the top of the mountain! No, the verb is not describing a physical action. Throughout the New Testament and in most of the Septuagint, it is used primarily in a spiritual sense. Thus, Peter uses it in his first letter to refer to spiritual offerings which are to be "carried upwards," which is to say, to God (2:5). This lifting up is certainly spiritual. When James tells us in his letter that Abraham "carried upwards" Isaac, he wasn't referring to the mountain but to placing him on the altar as an offering (2:21). Of course, Jesus was not offering the disciples as a sacrifice here, but he was carrying, lifting them up to God; he was bringing them into a particular spiritual elevation. The statement that the mountain was high is doubtless to signify the greatness of this elevation.

Implicit in the verb is that this lifting up is experienced in prayer; we understand this insofar as any spiritual elevation is a turning towards God. Jesus and the disciples therefore went up a high mountain, praying all the while, certainly in the case of Jesus, who was lifting the disciples up in prayer, lifting them to God. However, if Jesus was lifting the disciples to God in prayer, this would give us to understand that the disciples were also praying as they climbed. When walking with someone who is praying, we are impelled to pray too, and this would be truer still when it's Jesus who is praying.

The rest of the sentence continues wonderfully in the same sense: "a high mountain," "apart," "by themselves"; all of this is conducive to profound prayer.

Matthew, who knew the Old Testament well, kept the same verb, which was used repeatedly in the Septuagint with the spiritual meaning (Gen 8:20; Judg 6:26 . . .). Luke, however, writing to former pagans who were practically ignorant of the Old Testament, went about things in an importantly different way, replacing *anaphérô* with two verbs, firstly, the classic term to express physical displacement upwards (*anabaïnô*, "he climbed") and then another to express the spiritual dimension (*proseuchomaï*, "to pray"). Luke had understood Mark perfectly and chose to make explicit what is implicit in Mark: "He went up to pray" (9:28).

The one difference between Mark and Luke is that Luke gives it to be understood that prayer took place once they had reached the top of the mountain, while for Mark, there was prayer throughout the climb, from the bottom of the mountain to the top.

"He was transfigured"

It's in this context of prayer that we find the verb that follows: "He was transfigured." The transfiguration was experienced by Jesus and the disciples in prayer and was therefore a real spiritual uplift.

We note that immediately prior to the transfiguration no one had spoken, which seems normal if they were all praying in their hearts; there was no word spoken during the climb and none when they arrived. Silence is very beautiful when filled by prayer. Apart from Peter, who interrupts his praying to make his rather futile suggestion, the others never stopped praying. This is important if we are to understand the transfiguration: this was not a curiosity but a spiritual event.

What is the meaning of "transfigure" (*métamorphoô*)? There are many things to say, and I am not putting them in any sort of order of importance. We can say first that the term is not found in the Old Testament and neither is "transfiguration." In Exodus, we find the incident when Moses' face began to shine on mount Sinai, but it is not said that Moses was "transfigured" (34:29–30). The Old Testament knew nothing similar to what the disciples were witnesses to here, so they had no point of reference for talking about it. This is important for us because Mark

152

himself didn't experience the transfiguration and had only Peter to inform him. He passes on the account he received from Peter, who must himself have had difficulty finding the right words to describe what he saw, especially since Jesus himself never discussed it.

Before Mark, only Paul had used this verb "transfigure" and not for Jesus but to describe us, Christians: "Don't conform to the present age but be transfigured by the renewing of the mind" (Rom 12:2) and "We all who, with open face, contemplate as in a mirror the glory of the Lord, are being transfigured into the same likeness, from glory to glory" (2 Cor 3:18). Paul is talking here about something internal, which is not a great help to us in understanding this account as reported by Mark because it is much more than simply internal.

Mark doesn't use the term elsewhere, only for this event, thereby emphasizing its uniqueness.

We should note that Mark uses the word in the passive: "He was transfigured." This could only be a divine passive. Who could transfigure Jesus other than God? So Jesus was transfigured by God, which enables us to deduce that God was very much involved, was at work in what happened without being named. We also need to note that the word "God" is not used in this passage. God is at work but is not named. The transfiguration is his work, and God was very much present on this high mountain but in an indescribable way. He works in a way that entirely escapes us, beyond our understanding; the transfiguration therefore belongs to the inexpressible, in the way that the presence of God is inexpressible. The whole account is of the same tenor.

God is not named and will not be named throughout this passage. Nevertheless, we hear him speak to the disciples, telling them that Jesus is his beloved Son (v7), so it is the Father who is speaking of his Son, and yet the word Father is not used; he too is to remain in the realm of the inexpressible. The one who speaks, Mark tells us, is "a voice"; this form of reference is really very discreet.

God is at work without being named; he is present at the moment he transfigures Jesus, and in reality he is, at this moment, much more present than appears; he was there from the beginning of the passage, there as they went up the mountain. To whom would Jesus have been addressing prayer if not God, his Father? God was therefore already present as Jesus and the disciples went up the mountain praying. He was listening to the prayers of his Son and of the disciples. It's in this magnificent context of a constant but inexpressible presence of God the Father that the trans-figuration took place.

Something of God was taking place; the transfigura-tion is certainly extraordinary to us, but, since it was of God, it must have been instinct with his humble love, a love beyond all other love, an inexpressible love. This is an account deeply immersed in the inexpressible.

The disciples were there simply as witnesses; by recounting the transfiguration, Mark makes us witnesses too. As we open our ears, our eyes and our hearts, God is present, fully present in a way beyond words.

The ineffable countenance

What exactly is going on? The description that follows the transfiguration itself will help us understand. Mark tells us of Jesus' clothing, which became an unequalled white: "His garments became shining white, whiter than earthly laundering could make them." With this extraordinary description, there is an aspect Mark passes over in silence. Mark doesn't describe Jesus' countenance, while his personal appearance is surely more important than his clothes. Matthew noted this lack and endeavored to complete the account with a description: "His face shone like the sun" (17:2). However, we will stay with Mark. We note that Mark finds unusual words to describe Jesus' clothes but not to describe his face; for him, it must have been too much to attempt. Why? Because this was the face of God, as far beyond his ability to express as God is inexpressible.

To understand this, we can put it alongside certain texts in the Old Testament. In the book of Isaiah, when God appears to him, Isaiah speaks about God's garments but not his face: "I saw the Lord seated on a throne, high and lifted up, and the train of his robe filled the temple" (6:1). Isaiah says nothing about his face because it was indescribable. Even the seraphim veiled their faces in order not to look on the face of God (6:2). No one, Moses was told, can see the face of God and live.

In a psalm we are told that God "wraps himself in light like a cloak" (10:42). Here again, we are concerned with God's clothing but not his face.

In the book of Daniel, God appears to Daniel, who describes God's garments and his hair, but says nothing about his face: "His clothes were white as snow and the hair of his head like pure wool" (7:9). Daniel goes so far as to describe God's hair but not his face, and, in the Old Testament, no one goes further than Daniel in his description of God.

The description is important for us. Among the authoritative manuscripts of Mark's gospel which include the account of the transfiguration, there is one which is relatively old, from the end of the 4th century; this is the Codex Bezae, which, supported by Latin and Syriac translations, tells us that Jesus' clothing was "white as snow." Darby[24] includes this detail in his translation of the transfiguration account: "His garments shone and became brilliant white, like the snow . . ." I don't know if this detail goes back to the original, but the description of Jesus' clothing is certainly similar to God's clothing in Daniel, which once again indicates his divinity.

All this is to say that if Mark doesn't describe Jesus' face, this is not an oversight; it is because he thinks of Jesus' face as the face of God and so touches on the inexpressible. For Mark, and for Peter who recounted the transfiguration to him, Jesus was appearing in his divinity. The three disciples saw Christ in his divinity and so were unable to say anything about his countenance, his face. Seeing Christ transfigured, "They were gripped by great fear," Mark tells us (v6), the holy fear felt in God's presence. It's so clear: Jesus is God.

It might seem strange, but this lack of a description of Jesus face is for me the most beautiful sign, the most beautiful attestation to his divinity. Mark couldn't have done any better in describing the inexpressible; the face of Jesus in his divinity escapes description. When Matthew says that his face "shone like the sun," it's pedagogically interesting for us to understand that it is dangerous to look into this face; but whereas Matthew is descriptive, presenting an image to our imagination, according to Mark, Jesus' face is beyond any image, comparison or description, beyond seeing, even with the eyes of the heart. God is beyond sight, indescribable, inexpressible, unimaginable . . . beyond everything.

24. JN Darby, Anglo-Irish, collaborated in a French translation of the Bible.

Mark reports all that he had been told by Peter, who witnessed the transfiguration. It's interesting to me that John was also a witness, right there on the mountain, but John doesn't include an account of the transfiguration in his gospel; I believe this is because he couldn't find words, the very person who tells us at the beginning of his gospel that "we have contemplated his glory" (1:14), and at the beginning of his first letter, "we have seen" (1:1).[25] John was unable to state the inexpressible.

I think we can now understand the nature of the transfiguration a little better. The Greek verb *métamorphoô* (and its noun derivative) is made up of a preposition *méta* which as a prefix means "with," "in communion with," and *morphé*, "form," "appearance," "type," "nature." The verb therefore means a form found "in communion with" another form, or again, a nature found "in communion with" another nature. In Jesus' case, this means his divine nature in communion with his human nature. Until then the disciples had only seen Jesus' human nature, but on the mountaintop they were enabled to see his divine nature, and it's because they had seen this divine reality of Jesus that his appearance became indescribable. The divinity of Jesus was so strong that even his clothing was transformed and became white, Mark tells us, white such as they had never been before. They became as white as the very clothing of God in Daniel's vision.

A passage from Paul's letter to the Philippians will help us in our understanding of the transfiguration; it's an important passage because we find the word *morphé* (condition, form, nature) twice: "Jesus Christ who is of divine *condition* . . . who stripped himself, taking the *condition*

---

25. The French verb in both instances is *contempler*.

of a servant and the likeness of a human person" (2:6–7). Paul tells us here that Jesus was God before he became a man, indeed a servant, so profoundly human that his divinity was no longer visible. On the mountain, God the Father intervened to transfigure his Son so that his disciples could see his divinity.

The miracle was performed by God, not for Jesus but for the disciples, as Mark specifies; "He was transfigured *before them.*" They saw Jesus in his divinity insofar as they were capable. Out of love for the disciples, God didn't let them see this divinity in its fullness, as it would have been their death. The miracle was adjusted, made proportionate, so to speak, to the spiritual capacity of the disciples.

This passage from Philippians importantly helps us not mistake the transfiguration. We might have understood that the man Jesus became God on the mountain and had thus changed his humanity for divinity. But Paul tells us that it's the reverse: Jesus was first God and he became man in his incarnation while losing nothing of his divinity, which had simply become hidden — until the transfiguration when his unseen divinity became visible to the three disciples.

Why was a miracle like this granted to the disciples? It wasn't as a spectacle but for their benefit, to lift them spiritually and help them through the Passion Jesus had just been telling them about (8:31), the Passion which was so difficult for them to understand and accept (8:32). With Jesus' death so inadmissible for them (as Peter's reaction demonstrates), God was enabling them to understand that the cross was not to be considered only in its human dimension when it would be really unbearable, but also in the crucified Jesus' divine dimension. To know that this crucified One was God is a grace that helped the disciples grow in confidence and enable them to believe that death would be conquered on the cross by Jesus in his divinity, with the victory confirmed on Easter morning.

The transfiguration was also a great help to the disciples if they were to put into practice the difficult saying they had just heard from Jesus: "If anyone wishes to follow me, let them carry their cross" (8:34). The "cross," so unbearable and even repulsive at first, becomes easier to receive if it is no longer the place of human defeat, but the place of Christ's victory in his divinity. To carry our cross is to live with our confidence in this victory of Christ.

In the transfiguration, God's wonderful solicitude for the disciples is manifest, bringing them strength.

Elijah and Moses

Mark continues his account by telling us that Elijah and Moses appear, conversing with Jesus. There's no doubt they were there as witnesses to the Old Testament, Moses representing the Law and Elijah the prophets, Elijah rather than any other prophet because his return had been announced as accompanying the Messiah (Mal 3:23).

"The Law and the prophets" is the way the Old Testament as a whole was described (Matt 7:12; 22:40 . . .). The presence of Elijah and Moses signifies the profound connection of the Old Testament with Jesus, who was the very one to fulfil the Law and the prophets. It was good for the disciples to see Jesus not as a disavowal of the Old Testament but as its fulfilment and, in a profound sense, its crowning event.

Moses and Elijah were perhaps also there to signify communion between the dead and the living; Moses had died and been buried (Deut 34:5–6), while Elijah had not died, having been taken up in a chariot of fire (2 Kgs 2:11).

The appearance of the two together would attest that they were now both as alive as each other before Jesus, the Lord of the living and the dead.

Their conversation might also leave us to understand that Moses, Elijah and Jesus knew each other already and that they were no more than continuing conversations substantially begun during their times on earth. This thought that Jesus had conversed with each of them in ancient times only makes sense if Jesus is God. When Moses spoke with God as with a friend on the mountaintop of Sinai, wouldn't it have been Jesus he spoke with (Exod 33:11)? Wouldn't the same be true of Elijah who also conversed with God on the very same mountain (1 Kgs 19:9 ff)?

What did they discuss together? Mark doesn't say, no doubt because it's not our concern. I would have nothing further to say had Luke not told us that in fact they discussed "the exodus Jesus would accomplish at Jerusalem" (9:31). The word "exodus" here means the death,[26] but in a very positive way, as a passage, a departure (the meaning of "exodus"). Moses was well qualified to talk about an exodus, a departure from slavery into freedom. But Elijah too had something to say as a man who instead of death had experienced an extraordinary exodus, carried away by a chariot of fire. Moses and Elijah were therefore both well able to encourage Jesus as he considered his forthcoming death.

"Let us make three tents!"

This brotherly conversation must have set Peter somewhat at ease because he then interrupted, proposing to Jesus that they make three tents. No doubt he would have been better to desist! Kindly, however, no one responded.

26. KJV translates here "his decease which he must accomplish."

Peter here addressed Jesus as "Rabbi," not as "Lord" or "my God," as would have been more appropriate (17:4). It's strange to see that Peter apparently forgot the divinity of Jesus in calling him by this uniquely, strictly human term. Perhaps this is why Matthew thought it best to replace "Rabbi" with "Lord," more suitably (17:4). In fact, I believe that Peter was not so much mistaken as wishing to reassure himself and cling to Jesus' full humanity since, in reality, he had been "gripped by very great fear," as Mark notes (9:6), and so was well aware of his divinity.

"Gripped by very great fear"

"They were gripped by a great fear": the word used here by Mark for this fear is very strong, *ekphobos*. This is a very rare word, used as a superlative of *phobos*, "fear." Elsewhere in his gospel, Mark uses the verb form many times, among others for the disciples when Jesus calms the storm (4:41) and when he walks on the water (6:50). Only here and nowhere else, Mark prefers to use *ekphobos*, which is much stronger and in the rest of the Bible is used to denote a reaction to God (Deut 9:19). When Mark uses it here, it's to emphasize the divinity of Jesus.

In the boat, Jesus was at pains to reassure the troubled disciples (6:50), but here he did nothing. In fact, there was no need to reassure the disciples because a cloud was going to do so!

"There came a cloud"

"There came a cloud": the cloud came and then, in just the same way, there came the voice. The two are presented by Mark in the same way, with the same verb "come" and the same lack of specificity because there is no definite article: "there came a cloud . . . and there came a voice."

Although this is not always made clear in the translations, it is significant that Mark attributes the same importance to the cloud as to the voice. We know that *the voice* is an apophatic way of speaking of God, similar to *the Name* in Judaism, and it does become immediately apparent that this is God the Father. How are we to think of this cloud which Mark puts on the same level as the Father?

On this point, the Church Fathers are unanimous: the cloud designates the Holy Spirit, who alone could be equal to the Father. Mark presents the Holy Spirit here in as veiled a way as he does the Father, each of them with a noun without the definite article, "a cloud," "a voice." In proceeding like this, Mark continues in the realm of the inexpressible which is as suitable for the Holy Spirit as it is for the Father. What is there that enables us to recognize the Holy Spirit here?

Firstly, the scene of the transfiguration strongly resembles the scene of Jesus baptism, where the Father is heard to speak an almost identical phrase, and where the Father's involvement was accompanied by the presence of the Holy Spirit (1:9–11). The form of a dove revealed his presence at the baptism, and here, a cloud. There, the Holy Spirit was silent and the one thing he did was descend as a blessing. Here too, he is silent, and his one action is to "cover with his shadow."

The verb épikiazô ("to cover with his shadow") used by Mark here is very rare and, apart from the parallel passages in Matthew and Luke, is only used once elsewhere in the gospels, and then in a significant way, being used with the Holy Spirit as its subject. The passage in question is when the angel Gabriel announces to Mary that the Holy Spirit will cover her with his shadow (Luke 1:35). The action is very protective and reassuring. Here at the transfiguration, it means that the Holy Spirit will dissipate the disciples' fear, comforting them.

The cloud comes to cover with its shadow not only the disciples but also Jesus along with Moses and Elijah, uniting them in perfect communion. In this way there was a silent response to Peter, who could never have brought them all together with his three tents! The Holy Spirit alone was a shelter to them all.

The inexpressible presence of the Trinity

It was then that there came from the cloud a voice, the voice of the Father. Before we examine what the Father said, it is important to note that we are in the presence of the Trinity: the Father was there, the Son too, as well as the Holy Spirit, all three in a wonderful communion. The cloud of the Holy Spirit enveloped both the Father and the Son. The Trinity is there, discreet and sovereign . . . Which is as much as to say that Mark is engaging us in contemplation beyond words . . .

This contemplation can only grow when we note that the cloud enveloped Moses and Elijah as well as the disciples, all of whom were therefore not outside the Trinity, at a distance, but in the Trinity. What a mystery! We can only respond with silence as did the disciples from this moment. What a mystery and what a miracle too; right here we have the great miracle and mystery of the transfiguration. That the divinity of Jesus should be apparent is both an enormous miracle granted the disciples and an invitation to contemplate such a mystery. But that the Trinity be present and envelop the disciples is a miracle and then some, immersing the disciples again in the contemplation of another indescribable mystery. Nothing further was said; their fear had left, another miracle because being "gripped by fear" was very natural. The presence of the threefold holy God filled the disciples not with fear but with peace, enveloping them in an infinite love which cannot be expressed, a love beyond all other love. The disciples were in the cloud, at the heart of the Trinity. What a wonder! It was the silence of peace and love . . .

It was in this time outside of time that the voice of the Father came from the cloud . . .

Before we listen to what the voice said, I think we should take a moment to note that Jesus' prophecy was fulfilled: "Some here will not taste death before seeing the Kingdom of God come with power." The Kingdom of God is there in the presence of the Trinity who wraps the disciples in love. The Trinity came in gentleness, with the extreme delicacy of a cloud that appears silently. The power is the power of humble and inexpressible love beyond understanding. United at the heart of the Trinity, the disciples were in the Kingdom of God together with Elijah and Moses, the living and the dead . . .

"And there came a voice"

"And there came a voice": what was the nature of this voice? Was it a thunderous voice like "the voice of many waters" (Ps 93:4), or again, as we find in another psalm, a "Voice that breaks the cedars, that shakes the wilderness, that causes the hinds to calve and ravages the forests" (Ps 29:5; 8–9)? Or is it a voice like Elijah heard on Mount Horeb, "The voice of a murmur of silence" (1 Kgs 19:13)? Mark doesn't say, once more because it's just beyond words. When God speaks, only the person who hears can say how God spoke.

Underlining the indescribable character of this voice is the fact that Mark doesn't add any description. There "came" a voice, but what else? At the beginning of the gospel, in the wilderness, a voice "cried" (1:3); but here, what? As at the baptism nothing is specified. The mention of the voice is followed directly by the words spoken by the Father. The rest is beyond words: "There came a voice from the cloud: 'This is my Son . . .'"

In the parallel account, Matthew adds a verb that introduces speech: "a voice *saying*" (17:5). Luke does the same (9:35). The addition shows that Matthew and Luke were not attentive to the features Mark was at pains to emphasize as inexpressible.

The way Mark remains in the realm of the inexpressible in a scene which is full of the mystery of the presence of the Trinity is thoroughly admirable. The Father is not named, neither as God nor as Father, but is very much present. The Holy Spirit is not named, while he too is very present, suddenly filling the place; the cloud both reveals and veils his presence since he remains unseen, hidden in the cloud, just as the Father remains unseen, hidden in the cloud. Only the Son is named, more often indeed than normal: Mark names Jesus four times (9:2, 4, 5, 8), which is a lot for such a short passage. No doubt this is to remind us of the full humanity of Jesus in an account where we might forget this.

The Trinity was present, offered to our contemplation. We understand well enough that contemplating does not mean seeing openly because the Father and the Holy Spirit remain unseen. Nevertheless, the Trinity is here to be contemplated with the eyes of the heart.

"This is my beloved Son"

"This is my beloved Son, listen to him!": the voice says nothing more, but the little that is said is of immense importance. The statement strongly resembles that made at the Jordan, at Jesus' baptism (1:11), but in reality, it differs considerably. At the baptism, the voice spoke to Jesus: "You are my beloved Son"; here, it no longer speaks to Jesus but to the disciples, speaking to them about Jesus: "This is my beloved Son." The continuation, absent from the baptism, calls on the disciples to listen to Jesus: "Listen to him!"

It's so wonderful that God should speak in this way to the disciples; this is the first time for such a thing to happen and isn't repeated anywhere in the gospel. It's an extraordinary gift the disciples receive from God. They are recognized, afforded importance and welcomed on this mountain where they had come without knowing why. They had let themselves be led by Jesus, who had "carried" them as they went up. It was a real spiritual advancement to hear God speak to them in this way.

"This is my beloved Son." When Jesus asked them, "Who do people say that I am?" (8:27), the disciples answered with what they had been hearing. Jesus then asked them what they themselves thought, but he held back from asking them another question, "Who does God say I am?" And now, high on the mountaintop God himself had just revealed to the disciples who Jesus was for him: "This is my beloved Son."

"This is my beloved Son": this revelation is so much more wonderful because it answers questions to which the disciples hadn't known how to respond. The day Jesus healed the paralytic, the disciples learned that the scribes had been asking about Jesus, "Who is *this* to speak in this way? He is blaspheming" (2:7). The disciples hadn't known what to say; but now, the answer was being given them by God himself. No, he wasn't blaspheming: this was simply the Son of God.

On another day, in the Nazareth synagogue, the disciples had heard the question, "Isn't *this* the carpenter, Mary's Son?" (6:3) They didn't know what to say, but now they knew: this man was both the Son of Mary and the Son of God.

Finally, the disciples would remember the day they themselves had asked and not known how to answer, "Who is *this* that even the wind and the sea obey?" (4:41) Now they knew . . .

Mark's method of composing his gospel is very fine. He carefully reported each of these unanswered questions, retaining in each the same word *"this"* (*houtos*), and then using it again here in the words of the Father, *"This* is my beloved Son."

When Peter spoke up at Caesarea, saying to Jesus, "You are the Christ" (8:29), Jesus didn't comment, but simply commanded the disciples not to speak of it to anyone. Perhaps Jesus wished to wait until the disciples heard God's point of view. Humbly, he hadn't wished to confirm Peter's confession, leaving it to the Father to confirm it himself. Now it was done, with an important precision: to say "you are the Christ" continued to correctly mean "you are the Son of David in your humanity" (cf 10:47), but also and equally "you are the Son of God in your divinity."

The beloved Son

One day, the disciples had also heard unclean spirits . cry, "You are the Son of God," as they threw themselves down before Jesus (3:11). The disciples had good cause to be troubled because Jesus had very severely rebuked the spirits, forbidding them to speak. Why? Hadn't they spoken the truth? Isn't this just what God said too? Well, no! The difference is very great. The unclean spirits had not said the most important word, "Beloved." The whole difference is in this and it's huge. The unclean spirits were a thousand miles from respecting the inexpressible love of the Father for the Son since they denied this love, rejecting and opposing it. They didn't welcome, contemplate or celebrate this love. They were far from being contemplative when it comes to the inexpressible love of the Father for the Son; they were deniers and adversaries of this love. The truth is in the mouth of the Father: "This is my beloved Son."

Nevertheless, the unclean spirits "prostrated" themselves as they said that Jesus was the Son of God (3:11). This is so, but I believe we can consider their prostration as a masquerade since it is loveless; a masquerade like this confession, without love for God, is a lie, and no less a masquerade than the prostration of the soldiers before Jesus in Pilate's court (15:19).

We have already discussed the word "love" in its noun and verb forms, but not the adjective "beloved," so it's a good topic to look at here. The adjective form is found three times in Mark, each time to describe Jesus: here, at the baptism (1:11), and in the parable of the vinedressers (12:6). Only God and Jesus use the word, as though it is higher than any other adjective, and indeed it is. Only the Father and the Son pronounce it because it only has its real profundity on their lips; ours are impure. We can of course use the word, and I do, but when we say that Jesus is beloved we should not forget its profundity and that, if we are able to say it lovingly, this is a grace given by the Holy Spirit who says it to us first. It is the Holy Spirit who enables us to confess in truth that Jesus is the beloved Son of the Father. This is also why Jesus silenced the unclean spirits: by saying that Jesus is the Son of God without saying that he is the beloved, they offend the Holy Spirit who alone can rightly use the term.

The word "beloved" is pronounced here by the Father in the presence of the Son and from within the cloud of the Holy Spirit; it's there, in the Trinitarian reality, that this word more than any other word, has its true depth. "My beloved Son": these words carry the depths of the Father's heart and are of unfathomable profundity.

The disciples had heard the Father speak of the Son in the cloud of the Holy Spirit, and so, enveloped in the mystery of the Trinity, they were silent and contemplative . . . How blessed they were! High on the mountaintop, after the Father speaks, there is silent, unfathomable communion between the disciples and the Holy Spirit . . . A profound and wonderful silence!

And we, the beloved children

But aren't the disciples just like us, aren't we beloved children of God as well? Of course! Paul himself says so: "The Spirit witnesses with our spirit that we are children of God" (Rom 8:16). Jesus too says: "The Father loves you" (Jn 16:27). If Mark doesn't talk about the love of God for us, it's because for him the word love is so great as to be beyond words. In his gospel, God speaks of his love for his Son only here on the mountain in the context of Trinitarian love, in the unfathomable depths of the Trinity, and at Jesus' baptism in the same Trinitarian depths (1:11); God doesn't speak like this to anyone else, as though outside the Trinity the word loses any exactitude. With this in mind, insofar we as are not gripped by the depth of Trinitarian love, we shouldn't use the word "love" excessively because we devalue and perhaps even profane it. Love is so often rendered banal and profaned.

What are we to say about God's love for us when Mark never lets us hear of it from God himself? I believe that by proceeding in this way, Mark was prodding us not to want so much to hear God say he loves us as to discern the love God has for us in our experience. To say, "I love you," is facile, but to manifest love concretely is something else, and it's this we find in the gospel. Here on the mountaintop, God doesn't speak to the disciples of the love he has for them, but he does demonstrate it in many ways. How so?

When the people of Israel heard God speak to them from mount Sinai, it was terrifying; the mountain was on fire; the people had such a fear of dying when they heard the voice of God that they wanted to keep at a distance and not hear it any more. They then said to Moses, "You speak to us and we will listen; but don't let God speak to us because it will be our death" (Exod 20:19). There is nothing of that here; the fear had left the disciples and they no longer felt in the slightest danger when they heard the voice of God. They were sheltered by the cloud that covered them in its protective shade. I believe that the security the disciples enjoyed was provided by God who was thus manifesting his love for them.

When the disciples had reached the mountain top, God didn't speak to his Son, to Moses or to Elijah, but to them and to them alone. They were wonderfully welcomed, greatly honored by God. Here again is a sign of God's love for them.

When he says to the disciples, "This is my beloved Son," God, as we have seen, was responding to the unanswered questions deep in their hearts; they were being wonderfully instructed by him; again, this is a sign of God's love for them.

At Jesus' baptism, God addressed his Son and the words came from heaven (1:11); here, he speaks to the disciples not from heaven but from the cloud. God reveals himself as a God who is very close and even united to them in the cloud. Surely, such proximity is another sign of his love.

I believe that in all these signs the divine love Mark wants us to perceive is very evident. We also need to sharpen the eyes of our heart to see in the daily affairs of our lives everything that is given us by God as a manifestation of his love for us. While God may not always say that he loves us, he is constantly demonstrating it. Our place is also to ask the Holy Spirit to help us discern every little sign of God's love.

"Listen to him!"

The final words spoken by God on the mountain again merit our full attention, especially since they require a response: "Listen to him!"

"Listen to him!" God is really astonishing! Even when he has three disciples fully disposed and happy to listen to him, God doesn't say, "Listen to me," but "Listen to him!" He had only spoken a few words and could easily have spoken more, but no! He preferred that Jesus be listened to, that Jesus and not the Father be heard! To their surprise, the disciples discover something they perhaps couldn't have expected, a Father who humbly effaces himself and gives place to his Son. What a humble Father! Perhaps it is also a surprising discovery for us, one that plunges us into contemplation not of the Son but of the Father. The disciples had already understood how humble the Son was; here they discovered that the Son is the image of the Father.

Mark continues his account, telling us that after hearing the voice of the Father, the disciples looked around and saw only Jesus. Moses and Elijah had disappeared. The disciples now had eyes only for Jesus, who no doubt they saw very differently, as they had never seen him before. They were ready to follow him and to listen to him — as never before.

"They saw only Jesus": this last statement is wonderful. There is a paradox: they saw only Jesus, but the Father was still there. The Father joined in the pervasive silence after speaking, but his silence was not absence. Seeing Jesus alone doesn't mean the Father is absent. The Father is always where the Son is because they are inseparable; the Father remains unseen but he is invisibly present in the visible Son. "Whoever sees me sees the Father," Jesus says (John 14:9); "The Father is in me and I in him" (John 14:10). The cloud might have dissipated, but the Holy Spirit was still present, also unseen, totally available, inseparably united to the Father and to the Son. When Jesus was alone, he was alone with the Father and the Holy Spirit, inseparably united to them.

"Listen to him!" The disciples' surprises were not over. The moment the Father cedes to the Son for him to speak and be heard by his disciples — the Son says nothing! Jesus still hadn't spoken to this point. He had said nothing throughout the ascension of the mountain; once they reached the summit, he still said nothing, and when the Father fell silent for him to speak, he still didn't. What a surprise! How could you now listen to someone who wasn't speaking? Understanding the problem in the disciples' hearts, the Father, always humbly and with love says this:

Listen to the silence of my Son because in his silence there is plenty to understand, perhaps more than in his words. His silence speaks, and speaks in a way beyond words since the most beautiful things he has to say to you are beyond words, inexpressible. The most beautiful thing is his love. He hasn't yet spoken to you of this because what he might say is beyond words, in the infinite depths of mystery. This love in its unfathomable profundity cannot be spoken because it is the profundity of the heart of God. But don't be discouraged from listening; listen differently, with the ears of your heart, the ears the Holy Spirit gives you; then you will be able to understand my Son speaking of love, but with other than human words.

Listen firstly to all he has already told you in this way, and this will help you listen to all that follows. Listen closely with the ears of your heart and you will understand that everything he has told you to this point is filled with his inexpressible love. But perhaps you haven't understood this? Do you remember the day he called you, there beside the lake? Did you see how his eyes shone with love (cf "see" in 1:16 and 19)? In his look there was his love; it is this that must be understood, not the love he speaks with his lips but the love in his eyes. It was this Elijah understood in the noise of silence on mount Horeb (1 Kgs 19:12). Jesus' silence is as loud as the silence of mount Horeb; it is the same silence that he fills with his love and is so good for you to hear. Here you have already understood this in his silence. When he led you to the mountaintop, it was in silence, and his silence was prayer for you; he carried you with love in his silence, and it is this that you must learn to hear. Ask the Holy Spirit, the one who was also silent there in the cloud, and he will teach you how to understand my Son.

Do you remember the way he looked at the paralytic who came down through the opening in the house roof, the way his silence was every bit as full of love as his words of forgiveness and healing (2:5). Everything about him is love, his words and his silence, and everything you can understand of love in his words is also there in his silence. Did you hear the way he said to you, "I am," when he walked on the water (6:50)? He spoke with the same weight of love as the "I am" Moses heard at the burning bush (Exod 3:14). Did you listen when my Son broke the bread and gave it to you (6:41)? He said nothing to you; it was all silence, but did you understand the way his actions were full of love? Didn't you understand the look in his eyes when he gave you the broken bread? Exercise the ears of your heart because he will break the bread again for you and give it to you again (14:22); it will be good if you can then understand all there is in his looks and his actions. It will be the same when he washes your feet without a word; these are actions to which you will need to listen (John 13: 4–5). Everything about him, his actions, the way he looks, all his silences and all his words, the whole of his being overflows with love. Pay attention and you will understand his humble love beyond words. This is the way he needs you to listen. His love is so overflowing that you can hear it everywhere; nevertheless, pay attention: his love is so humble, so profoundly humble, that you will also need to be particularly humble to understand it. So, pray! Pray, asking for humility because the human heart is too sick to be genuinely humble.

Listen closely and you will also understand that his love, his humble love, is in each of his words, including those that are difficult to grasp. If you don't hear his love in his reproaches, pay attention; this means that pride has clogged your ears because pride prevents understanding, just as every spiritual malady prevents understanding of the love that is inexpressible. If you don't hear, then pray, pray again and come to him, humbly, and he will open your ears in the same way he opened the ears of the deaf mute (Mark 7:35).

If you have the impression you hear pride or vainglory in the words or deeds of my Son, then think again because you have gone astray; listen again to what he is saying as often as necessary, until you hear his love. If you hear poorly or not at all, pray without ceasing to the Holy Spirit and he will give you real hearing.

And now, my beloved children, go! You can go down from the mountain! My Son is waiting to go down with you. Just as he carried you here, he will carry you still, as he carries you always in his prayers.

Listen to him!

You are blessed, Lord Jesus,
you who are there with us in the cloud, so close to the
Father and the Holy Spirit,
so close to us too, perfect in your humanity;
you are blessed, you who offer yourself to our gaze in your
perfect divinity,
so far as our eyes can bear it.
We pray you, grant us the grace of your Holy Spirit,
that he come and be in us as we are in him in the cloud;
that he grant us deep listening, the listening of the heart;
that he come to purify our hearts of all that might prevent
us hearing,
that at last we might understand each of your words
in the depths of their love and humility;
that he grant us to hear even reproaches, your difficult words
in all their depths of love;
that he also grant us to hear your silences
and to understand your acts
with all the love your acts are charged with,
as is each look in your eye.
Lord Jesus, do us this grace, in your love for us,
to keep us from straying; we pray this of you,
of you our Lord and our God with the Father and
Holy Spirit,
now and always and throughout the ages. Amen.

Printed in Great Britain
by Amazon